Thinking and Learning Through Drawing

Thinking and Learning Through Drawing

In Primary Classrooms

Gill Hope

SAGE

Los Angeles • London • New Delhi • Singapore

First published 2008

SAGE Publications Ltd
1 Oliver's Yard
55 City Road
London EC1Y 1SP

SAGE Publications Inc.
2455 Teller Road
Thousand Oaks, California 91320

SAGE Publications India Pvt Ltd
B 1/I 1 Mohan Cooperative Industrial Area
Mathura Road
New Delhi 110 044

SAGE Publications Asia-Pacific Pte Ltd
33 Pekin Street #02-01
Far East Square
Singapore 048763

Library of Congress Control Number: 2008922550

British Library Cataloguing in Publication data

A catalogue record for this book is available from the British Library

ISBN 978-1-84787-039-1
ISBN 978-1-84787-040-7 (pbk)

Typeset by C&M Digitals, Chennai, India
Printed in Great Britain by The Cromwell Press Ltd, Trowbridge, Wiltshire
Printed on paper from sustainable resources

Contents

Drawing to think

People use drawings in a whole range of contexts; even people who say they never draw. Many adults make use of sketches in the course of their everyday lives, quite apart from the work-place use of plans and diagrams for buildings, electrical circuits, flow charts of productivity or traffic movement, or for layout and product design, for example:

- sketch maps are frequently drawn to give directions
- people can be seen walking around do-it-yourself (DIY) stores clutching sketches of ideas and diagrams of room sizes
- drawings are frequently used to aid explanations, of how to make or mend something
- doodling, especially when on the phone or in meetings
- demonstrating abstract relationships (for example, the new management structure).

Many people in all walks of life use drawings as a way generating, developing and communicating ideas. Such drawings are place-markers: they act as an anchor for evolving thoughts as they move towards a partially perceived end. These are staging posts on a journey of discovery as each idea unfolds into an externalized record of a blurry inner image as it gradually comes into focus. Drawings may be waymarkers on a journey towards understanding or resolution of a problem. Drawings may be springboards, place-marking, thought-holders, dynamic, evolving, informing and developing thinking.

But these drawings rarely get seen beyond their immediate context. They are redundant once they have served their purpose and, apart from professional designers who might want to keep them for future reference, these functional drawings are discarded. Even a genius like Leonardo da Vinci, whose drawn output was prodigious, scribbled drawings and jotted notes all over any odd piece of paper lying about and did not keep them in any order. However much we value these wonderful drawings today, it is clear that they were, for him, only a way of helping him think and jot down ideas about current or future projects, or just doodling and playing with ideas. It is possible at Tate Britain to request to view Turner's sketchbooks, which he kept as a personal visual library, but most of these are not on view to the general public, who see only the finished works hanging in the gallery.

The focus of this book is the way in which drawing can be used actively and dynamically to support, generate, develop and expand thinking and enhance learning. Often, those who have studied children's drawings have viewed them as finished products, statements of completed thought, crystallizing a frozen world view, detached from the context (physical, mental and emotional) that produced them. The aim of the book is to celebrate and explore the multiple forms of drawing which children do and can use in order to develop and record their thoughts and creative ideas, and to enable adults (especially teachers) to encourage and enable children to do so. The book aims to widen teachers' understanding of drawing and to equip them to enable children to use graphics as a powerful learning, thinking and communication tool.

This book does not attempt to say everything about drawing as a process for thinking and learning. It cannot: the subject is too vast, even limited to considering its use within the school curriculum for the 5–11 age group. Neither does the book give direct instructions on how to teach any specific techniques or drawing skills. There is some discussion on the tools of drawing, and a little advice on which tools to use and how to use them. The aim of the book is to provide starting points for thinking about the use of drawing of all kinds to generate, model, develop and communicate thought across the curriculum. The book aims primarily to do what drawing itself can do: to contain ideas that are taken on a journey of discovery; a journey whose end is not contained within the medium yet has enough packed into it to kick-start the creative process by making inner thoughts explicit and forming the basis for further thought, discussion and learning.

Defining drawing

A basic definition of drawing as a form of purposeful and meaningful mark-making would satisfy many people, but beyond that opinions divide. The obverse of this statement, however, that purposeful and meaningful mark-making is drawing, would be contested by many, since writing, mathematical notation, musical scores and other visual symbolic systems constitute marks made for and containing purposeful meanings, which are not 'drawings' in the usually accepted sense. Some thinkers and researchers would place handwriting, especially calligraphy, closer to drawing than a typescript, whereas artists who use drawing for recording ideas and observations which they ponder over, return to, interact with and use for preparatory thinking might find the inclusion of road signs in the same category as their deeply personal sketch books plainly offensive.

The word 'drawing' is one of those action words which can describe both a *product* and a *process*. 'To draw' is to purposefully make a mark; a 'drawing' is the result of that mark-making. The word 'purposefully' is important. Random dots, lines and squiggles that do not originate from human intention cannot really be classed as drawings. Children's scribbling is purposeful; they are exploring the effect of crayon on paper and developing their hand–eye coordination. Even doodling can be included, as it subconsciously helps maintain emotional equilibrium and reflects a concealed psychological state (compare your doodles in a boring meeting to those when you are getting cross about the issue).

The distinction between 'a drawing' and 'a painting' is hotly debated. Apparently, in judging the Jerwood Prize for Drawing, the judges are frequently drawn into discussion over what constitutes drawing in order to decide whether a particular entry is or is not a drawing. One judge's contention was that a drawing had a dialogue with the space on which it was executed, such that the areas left unworked formed part of the finished form. A painting, in contrast, he asserted, was completely covered with paint.

But where does drawing come from? Is it innate or learned? All infants scribble and make marks, often in places where parents would rather they did not. One family had to live for some time with a red biro line tracing a route all around the whole house. The word 'He-man' appeared mysteriously in pencil on my fireplace soon after my son started school. This desire to make a mark, to declare our presence can be seen in the caves of France and Spain. Whatever the true significance of the cave art of Lasceau and other places, the people of the Upper Palaeolithic were declaring 'We Are Here' in a way that the Neanderthals who lived there for millennia before them never did. The cave artists were Homo sapiens. To draw is part of what it is to be human. It is ubiquitous, multi-purpose, multi-faceted, multimedia, multicultural and multi-meaningful:

> ... the human mind is predisposed to seek similarities within and between its accumulating conceptions, and to assign these to categories ... (plus) the predisposition to assign symbols to represent conceptions, categories and relations. The use of symbols permits abstraction in inner thought, and the

externalization of thought for recording or communication purposes. (Archer, 1992: 5)

Drawings express relationships. These relationships may be physical (size, scale, position in space), abstract (expressing theoretical concepts) or analogue (the London Underground map). Drawings are not the same as pictures, although the two overlap.

Drawing comes from within, from an image held in the human mind. Even when engaged in observational drawing of an object placed directly in front of our eyes, our minds act as a filter:

> Man is *an animal that has developed symbolic functions*. However, *the map is not the territory*. Both physiologically and mentally, our inner maps, like sieves, only allow a part of the available exterior information to filter through. They present it to us as corrected proofs of a partial approximation. They are very diverse and divergent, from one person or from one group to another. (Fèvre, 2004: 47, my translation and italics)

This predisposition towards use of symbolism emerges early in life. The requisition of objects to accompany the fantasy role play of small children (an infant sitting in a clothes basket pretending to row it across the kitchen, for example) is foundational to the abilities which underlie the manipulation of symbols, including drawing. Those children who engage in rich imaginative play are good at visualization and hence are one step ahead on activities that rely on manipulation of symbolic ways of thinking. Those who do not play so imaginatively and make one thing stand for another do not manipulate symbols so readily, and so experience difficulties in imaging multiple solutions:

Drawing on the imagination

Although we may not be able to draw what we can imagine, we certainly cannot draw unless we can imagine. Humans actively construct alternative worlds, whether in our private daydreams or public storytelling, a quick sketch of the shelf for the bathroom or the design for the Pompidou Centre:

> The imagination: What is it? The mind actively constructing the not-here; the not-now, the not-me. The mind actually constructing actual worlds inhabited by actual others, others who breathe and bleed, think and feel. The mind constructing possible worlds inhabited by possible others. The mind constructing and furnishing the interior of one's own sensibility. (Emig, 1983: 177)

Drawings are visual representations of our inner images. As well as standing alone or beside other forms of meaningful mark-making, drawings may be placed over the top of or lie beneath other forms of visual representation. Drawings are not necessarily made on a flat surface. They may decorate a sculpture, or be graffiti on a railway bridge.

Architects frequently use drawing, not just as a means of symbolic representation, but to actively generate ideas (Goldschmidt, 1994). Their preferred mode of thinking often seems to be through drawing and fitting words around the drawings or even on Post-it notes stuck on top of the drawings. The indeterminacy, the woolliness inherent in drawing (missing lines, multiple contours), grants a level of perceptual ambiguity which, in turn, allows the mind to play with the drawing and seek out not only alternate readings, but alternative meanings that are allowed to continue to exist through the ambiguities of form. Artists do it too. The cartoon for Leonardo da Vinci's *Virgin and Child with St. Anne* (in the British Museum's Print and Drawing Room) demonstrates how Leonardo seemed to be trying out several different resolutions of the placement of the two women's legs in relation to each others'. He seems almost to be more at ease with the ambiguity than with the final resolution (on view at the Louvre, Paris). Perhaps making a commitment about the final form of the product was difficult for the Renaissance's 'ideas man' par excellence.

By occupying this middle ground between the imagination and the real world, even drawings of minimal clarity can be discussed and explored as if they were real. They extend and make visible the inner thought processes of their creator. By objectifying inner thoughts and images, the drawing enables these to be observed by the thinker. The imagination becomes visible and takes form. Changing and developing ideas now have something tangible on which to work, allowing review and reflection, return another day and with other ideas both new and old, which can be incorporated with the ideas recorded. The common thread is the need to record visually and graphically that which could not be considered, manipulated or communicated by words alone.

Drawing can be seen as a means of objectifying an inner image, as part of the interaction between the inner world of our mind's eye and the outer reality of the environment. It is more than just the product of a process, it is also part of the process. When we look at the role of drawing for designing, we are looking at a process whose interim stages are rarely preserved or valued except by the practitioner as a resource for future ideas.

There is a distinction between drawing as *product of* thought and drawing as *process of* thought. The first describes an artefact; the second a process. The first brings closure to the activity on the completion of the act of drawing; the second describes a way of recording thoughts in action. They frequently occur together, especially in the action of designing. Several completed drawings may form a chain of products which together map out the path that thought has taken. It is not an 'either/or' dichotomy, rather a 'together/and' interaction, which supports thinking in process and, through the creation of visible products, enhances reflection and evaluation of thoughts and ideas.

The Container/Journey metaphor

This metaphor forms the theoretical framework and conceptual underpinning of the book and, indeed of my understanding of the role of drawing for learning and thinking, as *container* for ideas which are taken on a *journey* across a surface (Hope, 2001). This model is adapted from Lakoff and Johnson's (1980) book *Metaphors We Live By*. The central tenet of their position is that new ideas and concepts are not just built from previously stored ones, but from the metaphors in which prior concepts are couched. The book centres on language and the way new concepts are built from previous constructs. Their main example throughout the text is the word 'Argument' for which they produced the diagram shown as Figure 0.1.

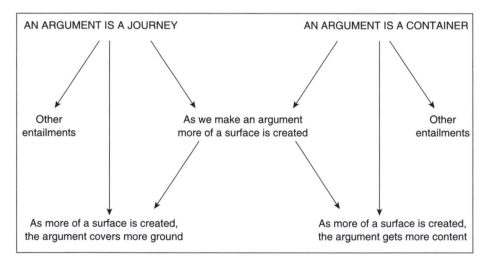

Figure 0.1   Extrapolation A (Hope, 2001), adapted from Lakoff and Johnson (1980: 96)

This model, with its specific metaphors of Journey and Container can be generalized to include all *process verb/product noun* pairs, for example, work, plan, draw, design, and so on (as shown in the Figure 0.2). Some of these verb/noun pairs do not share exactly the same word, but the metaphorical connection remains. For example, the verb 'make' has no

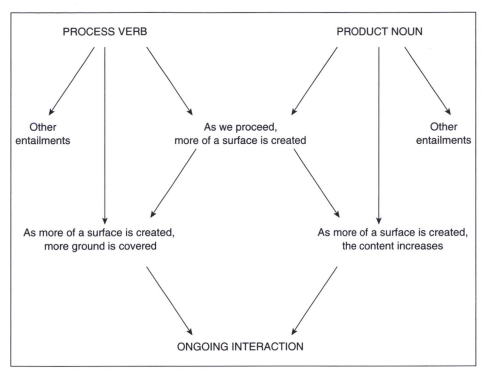

Figure 0.2   Extrapolation B (Hope, 2001)

directly attached noun, but the process of making and the object that is made have the same Journey and Container metaphors entailed in them. In making an object, we undertake a *journey* of thinking and planning and doing. The object we make *contains* all those thoughts and plans and actions.

The word 'drawing' fits neatly into the pattern (Figure 0.3). 'To draw' is a process which is a creative *journey* which we undertake. 'The drawing' is the thing that *contains* our ideas and perceptions. When we use drawing as a tool for thought, we take our thoughts, along with our pencil, on a *journey* and produce 'a drawing' which is then the *container* for those ideas.

In my development of Lakoff and Johnson's thought (Figure 0.4), I have reversed the relative positions of the two metaphors, because it is conventional to read from left to right, and I believe that in practice people begin to make a drawing that contains their initial ideas and then move off on a thought journey as they draw, changing and developing interactively as ideas develop, sparking off new ideas as existing ones take shape, and incorporating new ideas that emerge or are gleaned from other people and other sources.

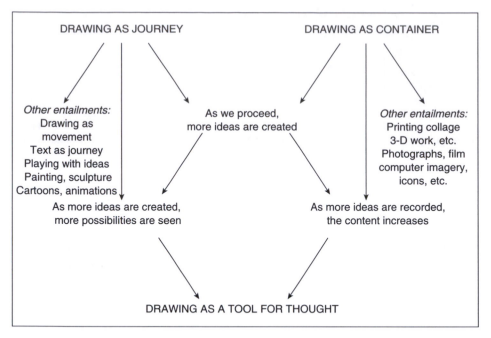

Figure 0.3   Extrapolation C (Hope, 2001)

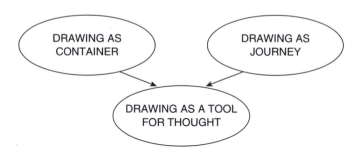

Figure 0.4   Container/Journey metaphor (Hope, 2001)

This model not only transformed my understanding of the role of drawing in supporting thinking, but also gave me a narrative in which to embed an explanation of the process of design drawing to Year 2 children (explained in 'Dimension 6: Drawing to design'). It is a useful metaphor of the process of drawing of every kind, not just for designing, since it assumes the symbolic, metaphorical nature of drawing itself. Drawing holds meaning contained within the form of the lines that extends beyond their physical mark on the page. The process of resolution of thought into graphic form is a journey involving exploration, ambiguity, clarity and compromise. It involves the use of symbolism as shorthand containers for complex emotional or psychological states or for social situations. It involves the movement of ideas across a surface, that can be reviewed, considered and provide yet more fuel for thought. This is as true of the small child's naive drawing of 'Daddy's house' as of the adult's sophisticated rendering of a multimillion pound community housing complex.

The Container/Journey metaphor is not spelt out in these words in every section so that readers become irritated with an overused mantra, but it is always there in the distinction between 'the drawing' (noun) and 'drawing' (verb) and exists as subtext to the use of the words 'product' and 'process' or in phrases such 'generate and develop ideas'. The development of the model is clearly focused in 'Dimension 2: Drawing to mean', in the discussion of *enaction* as the active and deliberate creation of meaning through process towards product through metaphor, analogy, semiotics and symbolism. However, whether spelt out or implied, the central tenet of this book is that all children's drawing in every dimension has this dual role: to carry their ideas on a journey of exploration that enables them to learn to think about a myriad new possibilities in every direction.

The dimensions of drawing

In order to impose some structure on an exploration and discussion of this ubiquitous, multi-purpose and multifaceted activity and to create a coherent storyline within the book, the examination of the multiple roles of drawing exploits the metaphor of the *dimensions* of the area of drawing. This seems a good metaphor that fits with the idea of journeying, as well as a convenient organizational tool. Drawings are created on a surface, which, whether flat or curved, is treated as two-dimensional in the act of drawing. The surface on which the drawing takes place has an area across which the drawing expands and is mapped as the drawing implement moves across it, exploring the space and leaving a trail of its passing. Crossing and joining lines breaks up the surface area into smaller spaces that convey meaning, feeling, knowledge, insight and inventiveness. The word 'dimensions' seems to express this sense of exploration of area, of moving about within a wide plain. Dimensions can spread. They define boundaries but enclose areas that may be full of possibilities. Expanding dimensions multiplies area. Thus, to talk about drawing and its purposes in terms of mapping dimensions seems to have a holistic sense of integrity with the subject matter and the Container/Journey metaphor. Each area of the book explores a different dimension of the use of drawing.

The name of each dimension begins with the words 'Drawing to …' which not only express purposeful activity but also direction, travelling, going somewhere that is, perhaps, exciting, exploratory and where the imagination and emotion have not been before:

Drawing to play
Drawing to mean
Drawing to feel
Drawing to see
Drawing to know
Drawing to design

This choice of organization conveys the range of purposes for which drawing may be used. These purposes, of course, overlap and the process of drawing (whether producing a single drawing or series of drawings) answers several purposes. A book is an essentially linear device for organizing information, and as soon as a reader is presented with a list, the inference is that the list is sequential and that the early items in the list precede those at the end, and that its categories are discrete, not overlapping or entwined. There may also be the assumption that the author thinks the list is exhaustive. Neither should be assumed from the organizational device of this book or of its labelling.

The introduction that you are currently reading is sub-titled 'Drawing to think', suggesting openness, beginnings, first imaginings within the head. There is, throughout the book, an inevitable ongoing conflict between the drawing process and the drawn product. The final section of the book, 'Drawing to conclusions', brings the book full circle and yet also looks to the future.

Overview of the dimensions

Drawing to play

This dimension begins with the stories: stories about young infants' first explorations of making marks on paper. The connections between playfulness and creativity are established. The importance of having time to experiment with any media before being required to produce something interesting or creative is asserted. An overview of drawing materials is provided.

This dimension is about discovery, about finding out how to use different materials and techniques at any age. Although beginning with the infant's first attempts at mark-making, this dimension stresses the importance of play, not just as a childish characteristic, but as an essential prerequisite to creativity. Finding out how to handle materials, mastering techniques, exploring different media is essential for 'possibility thinking' to use Craft's (1997) term, as is the development of a playful, risk-taking disposition. Playing with ideas, taking ideas on a journey of discovery towards an effective outcome, is only possible through developing the knowledge of the materials and techniques that will contain and express them.

Drawing to mean

Drawing is imbued with meaning surprisingly soon after its first appearance in the child's repertoire of activities. This dimension explores the meaning which drawing is given and can express and the way in which it stands as a visual metaphor for ideas in the head and perceptions of the observed world. Also considered is the way in which pre-school children combine both drawing and writing as their understanding of symbolic recording systems develops.

A major thread which is explored in this dimension is the role of metaphor and analogy and the way in which drawing is 'seen as if' it were a real object or scene or as a representation of knowledge about relationships between abstract ideas. Drawing acts as a bridge between the inner world of the imagination and reason and the outer world of communication and sharing of ideas. This is true both of the products of drawing (the containers of the ideas, perceptions and relationships) and of the process (the journey undertaken in exploiting and developing the analogy or visual metaphor).

Drawing to feel

The discussion begins with a consideration of the sensual appeal of the media, the feel of crayons and the smell of paint. It considers the sense of fulfilment and well-being generated by creative endeavours, the role of pattern, music and poetry. The range of emotional states that are generated by and perceived through drawing are explored, including a discussion of drawing and spirituality.

Immersion in the process of drawing can significantly impact for good the child's sense of well-being through the intensity of involvement in a process that does not pass through the language receptors of the brain but engages directly with the emotional triggers. Directly expressing a full range of emotions through drawing is difficult for young children, whose repertoire with lines and forms is limited through inexperience and practice. However, this should not deter teachers from expecting children to explore feelings and emotions through drawing. The form that the drawing takes may contain, to adult eyes, little of emotional impact, but for the child the process of thinking through a situation or of empathizing with others may be a journey of exploration of emotional and spiritual affect.

Drawing to see

This is not an explanation of how to get children to produce realistically lifelike portraiture or landscapes. This discussion is about seeing as understanding, and about expressing and exploring that understanding through drawing. The reasons for young children's production of canonical drawings are discussed together with the development of children's locational drawings. The sub-genres of observational drawing are considered to illustrate the range of demands made on children's understanding.

The discussion is placed within the framework of the developments of adult art across the past 100 years, which has witnessed deep changes in how the verb 'to see' is interpreted in relation to drawing and painting. This should be reflected in the expectations that teachers have of children's art. 'Seeing as' in Wittgenstein's (1969) sense of the word is a making sense, a perceiving and understanding, of making connections and linking new observations to prior knowledge. Requiring children to aspire to produce lifelike images that contain no more than poor camera shots of the world around them is to offer a poor model of observational drawing and denies children the richness of experience of travel through the possibilities and potentialities of the multiple genres of locational representation.

Drawing to know

This dimension covers the use of drawing to plot abstract concepts such as mathematics, to understand the form of things through geometry, and to find a path to other places through map-making. This is drawing at its most cerebral and yet its most basic. Simple line diagrams are used to develop ideas and communicate them to others. Puzzles and problems can be solved by seeing them as sharing common topographical forms.

Line drawings that are used to plot relationships can enable the modelling of concepts and complex abstract ideas. These make the topological form of the puzzle or problem visible and enable the classification of like problems through conceptual mapping. A relatively small set of these mappings can be used to support children's thinking and to develop their abilities in perceiving the underlying structures of problems which at first sight appear to be quite different.

Cartography, the plotting of maps of the physical, geographical world enables children to develop a sense of place and a means by which they can image the spatial relationships between different locations, whether on a large or small scale. The journey taken in this case might be literal.

Drawing to design

The final dimension to be discussed is design drawing. Not because it represents the zenith of children's capability but because a depth of understanding is required about the way things work and the way drawing can be used to represent, generate and develop innovative ideas. The use of the Container/Journey metaphor with a class of Year 2 children is explained and the way in which this enabled them to use drawing as a tool for design thinking is discussed.

In the concluding section of the book 'Drawing to conclusions', the main points from each dimension are drawn together and some ways forward for teachers are suggested.

Drawing across the curriculum

This book asserts a holistic view of its subject matter. There are no sections called 'art', 'D and T', 'science' and so on because these are in many cases false divisions. The problem with seeing disciplines or curricular subjects as discrete entities is that this creates the urge to define the boundaries of the subject into *is/is not*. For instance, where mathematics begins to overlap with art or geography, the temptation is to pull up the drawbridge and declare that this area of the subject is no longer mathematics. By this thinking, mathematics is 'pure'. It is 'hard' and abstract, with little relationship with other areas of life. The UK Numeracy Strategy, for instance, by defining the mathematical content of the curriculum, has frequently led to the delivery of a subject from which has been expunged any overlap with other curriculum areas, so that the content is concentrated on arithmetic and algebra, with little emphasis on geometry, visual patterning and conceptual spaces. This defining of mathematics as numbers has excluded much of the material that forms the cornerstone of twentieth-century mathematical research into pattern, symmetry and chaos that children find exciting and stimulating.

This is equally true of other areas of human knowledge. The more strictly the boundaries between one discipline and another are established and defended, the more the application of one way of thinking to another area of endeavour is precluded. This is worrying because many great leaps forward in human knowledge have been achieved by those whose training or background was in one disciple and who then moved into another, taking with them the insights and metaphors of the former. Keeping the boundaries tightly guarded means that useful metaphors cannot creep across. If Lakoff and Johnson (1980) are right, that all human knowledge is created through application of metaphor from the already known to the new encounter, then it is fluidity across the boundaries that we should be encouraging in our children and young people, and ignoring the hand-wringings of the gatekeepers of the subject disciplines.

A new world in a new century needs new ways of thinking. The gigabytes of computer power now at our disposal should help us to realize that the old linear way of recording ideas is past. Gardner (2007) identifies 'Five Minds for the Future' for the twenty-first century. Pink (2005) looks for 'A Whole New Mind' for the 'Conceptual Age'. Meanwhile, schools chug along much as they have before, snowed under with government directives and repeated calls for returns to old ways of doing things ('Back to Basics' and other similar cries). Why, bewailed Toffler, in 1970, do our schools still 'crank out Industrial Man' (p. 361) when 'Johnny lives in the hurricane's eye of change?' (p. 371).

This book is unlikely to radically change the curriculum but its aim is to expand teachers' thinking about how children's ideas are generated and recorded. In many areas of the curriculum, children's thinking and learning could be enhanced by using drawing to support thinking in conjunction with other ways of recording and developing ideas. Drawing is a powerful and accessible yet frequently under-utilized means of enabling children to learn and understand the ideas of others and to effectively generate, develop, draft, express, expand and communicate their own wonderful ideas.

Some of the functions of drawing for learning and thinking

Multiple uses and applications of drawing for learning and thinking are explored throughout the course of the book, frequently in juxtaposition. The following list indicates the key uses of drawing as a process for learning and thinking:

generating ideas
developing ideas
developing personal response
investigating form

understanding function
modelling ideas, concepts and relationships
clarifying ideas, observations and relationships
representing abstract concepts
mapping relationships
analysing concepts
establishing patterns
developing understanding
questioning observations
manipulating key concepts and relationships
developing narrative
communicating to others.

This will involve the development of:

observational skills
discernment of similarities, differences and patterns
recognition of scale, proportion, relationships
hand–eye coordination
motor skills
knowledge and understanding of materials, tools and techniques
development of visual literacy
language
evaluative and critical skills
formation of personal viewpoint
willingness to change and adapt
higher-order analytical skills
meta-cognitive reflective and analytical capabilities
multimedia communication skills.

The form of the drawn product may be:

sketches and first drafts of half-considered ideas
well-finished products that closely mirror an observation
random marks, lines, patches of colour
text items as well as drawing, including numerals and other symbols
analogues of concepts and relationships
expressive of deep emotion
purposefully dispassionate
possibilities for production in another medium
developing and communicating personal or shared meaning
exploratory of materials and techniques
part of a series that develops ways of communicating ideas

symbolic, semiotic, metaphoric, metonymic, analogical, allegorical, paracosmic
for private pleasure, a social act, or public view
any or all of the above.

None of these are exhaustive lists. Their purpose is simply to indicate the range of processes that drawing as a tool for learning and thinking can encompass.

Dimension 1

Drawing to play

The need to play is essential to human intellectual growth and emotional well-being. Children deprived of play through illness, hunger, trauma, abuse or other deprivation often demonstrate signs of emotional disturbance. The greatest of human minds, in fields as diverse as science, technology, art, music, religion, politics or philosophy, all play. They use the capabilities honed in childhood to imagine, dream, create, consider and invent new ways of solving physical, social, intellectual, aesthetic or spiritual problems. Playing with ideas is not just the highest form of human intellectual activity, it is also the most fundamental. It is where we all begin: to wonder, to think and to become independent rational beings. Although unable to articulate their thoughts, a babe in arms looking at the world over their mother's shoulders begins to want to play, to want more than the comforting rhythmic motion of mother's footsteps and the flickering light and shadows that pass by. Humans come pre-programmed to need to interact with other humans, to learn, to communicate and to invent. Coupled to language, purposeful communicative mark-making moved Homo sapiens ever further away from their nearest humanoid cousins until they became a separate species that dominates the world, for good or ill.

Playing with mark-making and imbuing it with symbolic meaning was a huge intellectual leap for humankind, probably greater than any other evolutionary development. It enabled out-of-range communication. It established the power of knowledge and its transfer to others. It externalized thought and enabled review and discussion. It enabled people to play with ideas in a new and powerful way. All these possibilities are learnt anew by each succeeding human generation, learning to create ideas and make meaning through marks on surfaces.

'Drawing to play', therefore, is the first dimension of drawing to be examined in this book because it is both the most basic and yet the most powerful use of drawing. The chapter looks first at the way in which infants and young children discover and use drawing to represent and investigate the world around them. It considers the ways in which children continue to hone these skills through play, and how teachers can enable them to develop their knowledge, skills and confidence in handling a wide range of drawing materials. The way in which children use their drawings to support their games is also discussed and, without too much straying into the territory of the dimension of 'Drawing to mean', how they exploit drawing's symbolic nature in so doing. The final section of 'Drawing to play' makes that bridge into the 'Drawing to mean' through focusing on the playing with ideas that underpins both the child's play and that of the greatest inventive minds, and how drawing can enable that most powerful of playing.

Vygotsky (1986) claimed that consciousness and control appear after a function has been practised unconsciously. There is truth in this, that fluency with any media is vital before it can be used for purposeful, creative action, but there is also a conscious determination to learn and master the function in the first place. Young children are so highly motivated to learn that this determination to mastery appears as play. They are committed to an activity and practise its skills with a joy that leaves adults standing. Never again in our lives do we learn so much about so many things so quickly. The continuation of that powerful, playful determination through childhood and adolescence into adulthood is the distinguishing mark of genius, whether at a personal or historic level of capability.

So, let us begin at the beginning …

Early mark-making

Around about her first birthday, Rachel stopped having her afternoon naps. This was irritating for her 3-year-old brother, Ralph, since this meant the disappearance of mum-and-son time, tucked up with books or on the floor with card games or at the table with crayons and paper. Now baby sister was awake and part of it. One day, mum had Rachel on her lap while Ralph played with pencils and crayons. Rachel reached out and mum handed her a pen with the lid on to keep her amused. She pushed it around like Ralph but it made no mark so she dropped it. Realizing what she wanted, mum gave her a pen with the lid off and pulled some paper within reach. Rachel pushed the pen around the paper and it made marks and she was visibly pleased with herself. She was doing what her big brother was doing. She was on her way to being a big girl.

In this anecdote of an infant's first use of a pen to make marks on paper are many of the ingredients that are part of learning to draw. First, it was social learning, part of the normal interaction between adult and young child. Second, it was initiation into the world of a more mature way of thinking and doing, and provided intellectual and emotional satisfaction. Rachel had analysed the nature of the process: pushing the pen around made marks on the paper. She had watched carefully how it was done and felt ready to try it for herself. This was an intellectual shift from wanting something someone else had and exploring it in her own way. This was purposefully copying exactly what someone else was doing in order to create the same effect. When she was successful, the satisfaction was obvious.

Rachel grew up to become a marine biologist, contributing to knowledge of the impact and management of fisheries. Ralph works in the world of investment banking, creating software to support international trade on the stock markets. Both are fluently confident in their ability to use graphics in a range of ways and situations, to support the development of thinking, communicate observations, generate ideas and demonstrate abstract relationships, in situations as diverse as home DIY, quick sketch maps to show where they live, to support hobbies and so on, as well as in their very different work environments. This taken-for-granted graphic fluency developed from the ability to make marks on a surface, combined with the later realization that these marks can hold and create meaning.

Early drawing activity is largely exploratory, purely experimenting with the process of mark-making, and not always with appropriate materials or surfaces. Playing with food is often an exploration of mark-making that does not always win the approval of parents, especially if this involves flicking. Running around on the beach trailing a stick is a more acceptable large-scale form of exploratory mark-making. Even children who are already drawing recognizable pictures will enjoy simply running and making a trail across this huge open space.

Frequently, young children become obsessed with specific aspects of the world, which they explore repeatedly. They have seen a pattern somewhere and want to discover its scope and potential. It might be looking underneath things (chairs, beds, stones, cars in the street) or through things (cardboard tubes, rolled newspaper, holes in fences) and may include something that embarrasses the parent or carer (the imaginary friend). Young children's mark-making often reflects these current interests and the building of the inner schema to which it is contributing.

Three stories of infants at around age 2 years, which follow, illustrate the way in which young children explore their current schemas through drawing lines.

Zheng

Zheng's inner imperative seemed to be taking a line on a journey, not necessarily making a mark, limited only by the size of the surface available. Trails were drawn with sticks, bike wheels, pull-along toys, or her imagination. By age 2 years and 6 months Zheng saw routes drawn out everywhere. Long journeys went along walls, across parks, through puddles, round trees, upstairs, downstairs and across and around pieces of paper. Her drawings seemed like long looping snail trails, around and around and across the page, the only breaks being where she unintentionally skipped the pencil across the page or where she decided to start a new trail on the same sheet.

Zheng was exploring paths, tracks and routes both on the macro and micro scale. She was developing a sense of space, line and loci. The marks she made on paper were analogues of the routes in her head. She was not consciously modelling any one of her journeys (or even a combination of them) but simply exploring the schema of 'journey' in another medium: crayon on paper.

Lloyd

At a similar age, Lloyd's passion was corners. He would 'hide' in them, feel them with his fingers, trace the meeting points of their inside edges, and play 'bo' round them. On a visit to his grandparents, he enjoyed whizzing his toy cars around the inside of a large wooden tray, like a race track. His granddad laid a piece of paper inside the tray to protect the picture from the car's wheels, which prompted Lloyd to run off, come back with a pen and trace the route round the edges, into the corners, across the middle, back and forth. He was highly animated, totally absorbed and thrilled at the result. Then, satiated, tray and paper and pen were abandoned and he was off to play a different game altogether.

Lloyd was exploring topology in a different way from Zheng. Seeing, in a flash of inspiration that would do credit to any adult scientist, that a pen could provide a permanent trace of the route, he explored and exploited it to the full. When he had completed his task he was triumphant: yes! Eureka! The process of drawing had enabled the bridge between outer reality and inner developing schema. By using drawing to support his thinking, Lloyd had creatively explored and internally conceptualized the role and properties of corners within an enclosed space.

Gurdip

In contrast, Gurdip (younger than Lloyd and Zheng, just short of his second birthday) was a dots and dashes man. Short sharp marks, preferably noisy or scraping, so that his mother had given him a thick notepad to absorb the impact of his penwork. Then he discovered going round and round, experimenting with speed, pressure of mark and colour, making really deep grooves in the notepad, round and round. Gurdip started humming then brmming to himself. His father asked 'Is it a car?' and drew one on the next sheet of paper for him. Gurdip did more round schemas on that sheet too and brmmed loudly. The noise seemed to please daddy more than mummy.

Gurdip had experienced an interesting encounter with an adult's perception of what he was doing that would sow seeds of thought for the future. His father assumed a connection to a car but Gurdip's brmming was just an accompanying doodling noise while he was absorbed with watching the satisfyingly deep grooves he was making into the notepad. He watched his father draw the car, stored it away in his head and carried on with what he was doing. He has realized how pictures in books are made. Adults make them with pens.

All three of these children had used drawing as an analogue for motor movement. Gurdip's father, in interpreting the purpose of the activity as symbolic, sowed the seeds in his son's mind of the symbolic potential of mark-making. For Zheng and Lloyd, this would come in a different way on a different day. Whichever route is taken by the child, whether through exploration on their own or aided serendipitously or intentionally by an adult, they have discovered a powerful tool for exploring and developing new ideas. Once they realize the symbolic potential of drawing, they have a new tool to aid and support their thinking, a means of expression with which they can play and experiment.

In affluent countries, because of the access that children have to drawing materials, drawing and language usually first develop within the same period of time (between ages 1–3 years). Where children do not have such access, researchers have reported that the kinds of drawings that they associate with pre-schoolers do not occur. When given pencils and paper, older novice artists progress quickly from initial experimentation with the medium to making images. Reports that these subjects have 'progressed' at an apparently accelerated rate without going through the 'stages' the researchers expect, based on young children's work in their home countries, should, perhaps be treated with caution. The desire to make representational marks is so ubiquitous that it is more likely that it is the kind of mark-making that is being sought by the researchers that is new to the research subject and that they are mastering at an (apparently) accelerated rate. In some cultures, infants' play is perceived as freedom to do as they like before learning, rather than as part of learning, as may be the view in the cultures from which the researchers have come. Some artistic traditions are passed down through a close-knit family apprenticeship system that does not include the rest of the population at all, and a child within such a family is expected to begin to learn this when they reach a certain age.

There is no 'natural' universal artistic development, despite attempts by some researchers to find and plot one. Young children play, experiment, adapt and learn to use a whole range of mark-making techniques from quite an early age but in different ways and in different cultural and social contexts around the world, and at different times. This book is culturally situated in the UK in the early years of the twenty-first century and should be read with this in mind. The references to school years and ages of children are related to that cultural situation, and recommendations for teacher action should be read as relevant within that cultural context. No universal prescriptions are attempted or intended.

Playfulness and creativity

Aided by the acquisition of language, infants learn to compare, contrast, differentiate and categorize their experiences and perceptions of the world around them. In their playing and their making, young children use their perceptions of the similarities between things, the analogies which they perceive all around them, sometimes by serendipity, sometimes by intent, using and combining them playfully and creatively to design a self-propelling shared world. In this, they are acting in exactly the same way as adult designers. Hence the term 'designerly play' employed by Baynes (1989) to describe such creative playfulness.

From about 1 year old, children begin to repeat back recognizable sounds which parents accept and reinforce and remember as their child's first words. The infant learns quickly that everything in the world has a sound label and all they have to do now is to find out what these all are, as fast as possible. That a mark made on paper can have a name label other than 'crayoning' or 'painting' but can be called 'dog', 'man' or 'mummy' is a considerable conceptual leap into symbolic abstraction, yet one which infants appear to take in their stride. It also changes the child's view of themselves, as agentic, as a creator of imagery. They have entered into a world parallel and yet very different to the world of playing with toys or even of spoken language. The mark they make on paper can be kept, examined, reviewed, displayed for all to see in a way that ephemeral speech and play cannot. Early meta-cognition, thinking about thinking, is aided by drawing.

In the beginning, the child is exploring mark-making for its own sake. As the idea dawns that these marks might represent something, scribbles obligingly may represent things for the adult enquirer. It is difficult, if not impossible, to know if this assigning of name to scribbling occurs to the infant without adult prompting since many, if not most, drawings are done with adult supervision at this stage. The fear of infants drawing on wallpaper, curtains and other household objects is too real to allow them access to drawing materials far beyond the watchful eye of an adult or older sibling. Thus the idea that drawings represent something is so early planted that it is realistically impossible to decide on its genesis. What is clear, is that almost as soon as infants decide that drawing can represent things, it does. Scribbles declared to be 'rabbit' appear to have long ears. Ones declared 'car' have wheels. 'Mummy' has a round head and eyes. It is a self-propelling iterative game. It is soon realized by many infants that adults will produce drawings for them, and the dialogue begins.

This dialogue is between a socially accepted way of representing people, houses, animals and so forth, and the child's desire to communicate. Young children are trying to learn these conventions just as keenly as they are trying to come to terms with a whole culture full of other social conventions. Very soon they realize that trying to be an adult straightaway is a bit too difficult right now, so they concentrate their efforts on becoming a bigger boy or bigger girl. By about age 3, apprenticeship into becoming a child in their own society is well under way and this includes learning how bigger boys and girls draw. This is learnt from older siblings, cousins, neighbours and friends at home, nursery and in school Reception classes. Drawing is just one of the games that young children play alongside each other.

As children's drawing capabilities develop, we see not only the development of their motor control of the mark-making tool, but also their growing awareness of their environment, both physical and conceptual. Early drawings are frequently of mummy, the car, the dog or family. Interestingly, few children begin their graphic career with drawings of 'me'. The evidence of early drawings suggests that the child has a very keen interest in the external world and very limited concern with representing their own image. They are committed to forming as clear a map of the world around them as possible and once they realize that drawing can support them in this quest, then they are hooked.

Abstraction and symbolism is the name of the game, not objective realistic representation. The 'tadpole figures' ('head' plus two legs) show all that is important about any human: consciousness and mobility. The 'head' represents the main axis of the human body and includes head and torso. Some investigators into children's drawings have asked inappropriate questions, such as 'Where is the tummy button?' and laid great store by the answers. Children are much more pragmatic than this. The early representations are symbols for people. Circles will do. Eyes and smiling mouth, denoting responsive awareness, come next. Legs are necessary to enable movement from place to place. Arms enable handling and holding. The head and torso remain undifferentiated because there are no major hinges involved. We do not swing our heads in the way that we swing our arms or use them to move about. Representing head and torso separately requires the ability to work out how they join. Necks prove difficult to get right, even for adults. Children tend to put arms in the 'right' place once they begin to represent clothing. Few figures with triangular skirts have arms coming from where their ears should be. Ears often appear at about the same time; jug-handles usually, as if the absence of arms from this place on the schema has left it wanting and needing to be plenteously endowed.

Making for play

When young babies learn to reach out to hold and explore the properties of physical objects, their earliest exploration is with their mouths. Although they have seen and wanted to touch and discover, their gaze is not necessarily focused on the object once they have it in their grasp. Familiarity with the tactile properties then leads to inquiry about other possibilities: sound, movement, colour, reflectivity. As babies become infants, the symbolic possibilities begin to be seen, through the appreciation of the analogies between one object and another, especially with regard to shape. A large box becomes a house, a garage, a space station, and so on. These play-props are part of the tool box for a game, a fantasy world which mirrors reality but occupies a different plane of existence. When the game ends, the objects that supported the fantasy game are discarded.

Properties can be reassigning as a part of play. Winnicott (1971) concluded that human play arises from our capacity to make bridges imaginatively between our own inner reality and the external world. Children combine objects from outer reality with ideas from inner reality to create a 'dream potential'. From about age 4 onwards, making the play-props may become more absorbing and satisfying than the final product of the effort and imagination. This can often include drawing and cutting out, both in preparation and as part of the play episode. These made objects do not need to mirror reality in every way. For instance, skis for teddy can be made from ordinary paper. The child is quite clear about the 'pretend' nature of what they are doing and can be confused by adults' expectations that these things are anything other than 'pretend'.

For instance, when children in a Year 1 class were asked to design and make a travel bag for the class mascot, they did not understand why it needed to have two sides and be able to really hold things (Hope, 2007).

Like playing, drawing involves the use of cognitive maps, ideas and representations to create a 'not yet fully perceived end, making meaning through action or imagined action' (Coghill, 1989: 128). Both Bailey (1971) and Coghill (1989) perceived curiosity as a spur to meaning-making, often embedded in, or projected into, aspects of physical reality that act as place-holders for thought and action, so they can be worked on or changed. As paper becomes alive through cut-outs and puppets, and children take the leap from drawing to animation, using their skills of role play and characterization, so they become involved in deep levels of designerly play (Baynes, 1989).

Children's use of drawn objects in play at this age is intriguing. If a child cuts out a drawing then the thing that is drawn changes its function and it can become an object for playing with in a way that uncut drawings do not (Kress, 1994). Cut-out drawn figures (for example, Figure 1.1) can become simple hand-held puppets that are made to dance across the table, talk or argue, and which might be made to lie down on 'beds', whether doll's furniture or drawn and cut-out for the occasion. Children do not usually draw a bed on a piece of paper and lay the cut-out doll on it without first cutting out the bed. Even less likely is for a child to lay an uncut picture of a person on an uncut picture of a bed as part of playing a game about a character going to bed. The drawing is not the act of creation of a play-prop, although it is the means towards creating it. The final act of creation is the cutting out, metaphorically freeing the puppet from its previous half-life as a line on a paper.

As the child talks through a cut-out character, so they verbalize their own thoughts about a range of situations. This makes their own thoughts and perpectives open to inspection, with the additional advantage over toys, because the child is aware that they have created a character. Whereas a teddy has a predetermined socio-cultural role or television toys have prescribed roles that children need to learn in order to play the game, paper figures, by their very transitory and child-created nature, allow the child consciously to look inside their own head for the role of these temporary guests in the game.

As the child plays, a storyline develops. The creation is moving, talking, reacting *in role*. The young dramatist has created the characters as well as the script. If other characters are needed, then they too can be made. Adults are more willingly engaged in fantasy play that involves cut-outs than in play involving toys and may help to create more characters, perhaps even ones the child has not thought of. Granny might helpfully

Figure 1.1   Cut-out drawn figures (Zara and Hayley)

hold teddy while the child is doing something else, but she will probably become fully involved in paper play. This adult involvement in fantasy actively supports and extends the child's imagination, while giving
social value to the child's playful activity. That such adult support in
role-playing is initiated through such transitory things as cut-out drawings is important. The temporary nature of such props for of-the-
moment games may mean that these cut-outs go in the bin within hours
of making. However, these temporary play-props are highly significant
in the child's creative and cognitive development. The child and adult
are together creating a world from nothing, externalizing the shared
imaginary world within their heads through making marks on paper
and, by cutting them out, making these marks into an object with character and/or purpose. Externalizing the imagination in a shared social
context enables the development of fantasy at a deeper level.

In any 'making for play' activity, whether alone or with others, young children around age 4–7 years, are prepared to do a fair amount of pretending. Realism is not their aim, but enough to satisfy the requirements of their imagination and act as a stimulus for further fantasizing. As children get older, they demand more reality from their toys and from the props that they themselves make (such as clothes for dolls, landing pods for space vehicles), which become ever more complex and demanding in their approximation to reality. The ease with which such toys can be purchased has, of course, been claimed to curb children's creativity and the criticism of children's television-related toys, especially, surfaces to public attention from time to time. Many children, however, especially in the 5–9 age range, seem to design and make additional props for their toys. This is parallel to the activity of adult designers, who usually start by looking at a range of ready-made products to discern where there is a gap in the market that they can exploit, while answering strict user demands and needs. This is not dissimilar to the young child realizing that their game character needs an extra hideout which leads to substituting a box or a drawing for the star-base they do not yet own.

Representational play, in which something that the child makes is used as a place-marker in their imaginary games, is part way towards fully internalized fantasy and inner dialogue. Language-mediated play, as the culmination of representational play, is essential for school success. Schomburg (2000) conjectured that one of the reasons that children with good representational skills do so well in school is that their opportunities for play are not cut off. They transform easily into the kinds of activities that teachers demand. Writing imaginative stories is easier for a child who has already tried out a whole range of self-made roles. In order to see themselves as writers, children need first to see themselves as storytellers. Cut-out drawn characters can help to bridge the gap between role play with toys and telling stories.

However, providing children in school or early years settings with ready printed line drawings to colour and cut out is unlikely to hit the spot. These are more likely to be seen as colouring-in and cutting-out exercises, and completion will lead to 'what next?' rather than to imaginary play. For instance, a teacher provided Year 1 children with a long strip of squared paper, to be coloured in and concertina-folded, to be called an Inch-worm with a string attached. It seemed to her to have potential to become a springboard for playful activity. Some children pulled them around the floor for a few seconds but most immediately put them away. The Inch-worm had come from the adult imagination, not theirs. In contrast, a few weeks later one child brought in a ghost made, at home with his childminder, from tissue paper bundled and tied around with a string. He recounted the making and demonstrated the potential.

The teacher provided a box of tissues and some cotton and offered to help tie the knots. Within ten minutes many of the children had a ghost which was dancing, talking and bouncing on its string. The difference? Empathy. The children understood and imagined Kieran making the ghost and could share the experience. They could take up the baton and run with it into their own imaginary world.

Child-initiated activities are vital for young children, both in and beyond early years settings, to develop their ability to play. Throughout the early years and into Key Stage 1, children need time and opportunity to develop their imagination through such free-play opportunities as well as more structured activities. Teachers and other adults working with young children are frequently encouraged to see play as a process, *a means of learning*, but are often less confident to assert that play is itself an *outcome of learning*, a skill which needs time, opportunity and practice. In order to use drawing or writing to develop creative and imaginative ideas, children need sufficient experience of letting their minds roam free and experimenting with thoughts, ideas and fantasies. Smith (1992) sees pattern-recognition as the mechanism which acts as the brake on fantasy running out of control. This pattern-recognition is socially learnt and practised in play, regulating the interaction between reality and fantasy. Thus children with a rich fantasy life are often the most adept at creative and design tasks. They have learnt to exploit mental fluidity, yet they have a strong sense of what would really work.

The relationship between children's play and the adult trait of playfulness was explored by Lieberman (1977), who compared the results of a set of 'Divergent Thinking Tasks' to a 'playfulness' scale for teacher assessment, on which she found correlation both for small children and adolescents, concluding that the quality of early playfulness affects the development of the adult personality trait. There is, claimed Lieberman, a direct link between the human characteristic of playfulness and that of creativity. Obviously, this does not mean that highly creative people are infantile or concerned with trivia. Rather, that they are constantly playing with ideas and seeking new ways of seeing the world around them.

Maintaining the capacity for inner fantasies is crucial to transform childhood playing into more mature forms of designing, whether the products be musical, artistic, scientific or just everyday living. Craft (1997) identified 'possibility thinking' as the core element in creativity, involving play, asking questions and motivation. For most people, this will come within Craft's 'little c' everyday creativity that enables them to be adaptive and spot solutions to problems or opportunities for action, but for some this will be what Craft calls the 'Big C' creativity of the highly innovative artist, scientist, designer, mathematician, musician, and so on. Playing with ideas through drawing is one way to enhance 'possibility thinking' by enabling each possibility to be recorded, stored and looked at again later.

Developing the necessary hand skills

To this point, the discussion has been focused on the child's cognitive and creative development through playing with drawing. Paired to the desire for an increasingly accurate representation of the human figure and the social world around them is greater control of the drawing instrument. For some strange reason, in educational settings, small hands are often given large, heavy and unwieldy brushes and chunky crayons with broad blunt ends, with which it is impossible to make an accurate mark. This is in contrast to the thinner colouring pencils, biros and felt pens and the brushes supplied with children's paintboxes that children use at home and which are far more in proportion to the size of the child's hand. Looking at the size of a 4-year-old's hand and scaling up to adult size quickly reveals the size, weight and thickness of the drawing materials that they are being asked to use. It is hardly surprising that they are limited to producing rough bold outlines or that they grip them with the whole hand.

Examining the hands of 4-year-olds quickly reveals just how much of the hand is still cartilage, rather than bone, and how flexible the joints are. This is vital for survival, growth and development. Bones cease to grow once they have calcified and young children take so many tumbles, knocks and bruises that serious injury would ensue if their bone structure was as stiff as an adult's. However, such a highly flexible hand makes tiny precise movements difficult. Attempting to line up a pencil to a particular spot on the paper needs considerable practice, to which the child is trying to add accurate movement of the pencil across the paper and apply an appropriate amount of pressure according to the tool used. Additionally, the child is also coping with a hand that is continuously growing (but not necessarily equally) in strength and size in all dimensions.

Many young children's reluctance to adopt a 'proper' pencil grip may be to do with physical discomfort or genuine inability to control the pencil's movement between their fingers (Figure 1.2). Most children adopt the standard grip naturally without pressure from adults as their hands mature. There are two common pen-grips that can be observed in use by adults for writing, and both right- and left-handers use them. The most common grip (and the one usually encouraged in school) is to have the wrist and arm in a straight line and the pen held within the outstretched but crooked thumb and first two fingers. The alternative position is to have the wrist at right angles to the fore-arm (Figure 1.3). There is no difference in neatness or speed of writing in either position, nor in other less

Figure 1.2   Straight grip

Figure 1.3   Right-angled wrist grip

common positions (for example, with the pen held between second and third finger). The standard 'straight grip', although good for neat hand-writing, is, however, very poorly adapted for drawing.

The 'straight grip' enables the ball of the hand to rest on the paper and the fingers to make very fine movements with the pen. Ideal, therefore, for right-handed writers, who can see what they have written as they write. Left-handers have the advantage of being able to see the line ahead and so do not tend to leave the line and go up in the air with their writing, but since they cannot see what they have just written, they need to remember where they were on the page, as instant review is more difficult. The use for writing of the 'right-angled wrist grip' seems more common among visual thinkers, both left- and right-handed. Being an easy grip for small-scale drawing as well as writing, these people have chosen for themselves the best of both worlds. Perhaps they naturally want to represent the world in a more fluid and less tightly defined way.

The development of children's handwriting has bearing on the development of their drawing style, since both are dependent on the maturation and development of muscle groups in the hand and the formation of neural pathways within the brain, and on the interaction between the two. Children who learn early to produce neat well-formed handwriting often develop a drawing style that reflects well-ordered visual schema, whereas children whose handwriting is less pleasing may produce looser more fluid drawings that suggest a greater ability to juggle uncertainty of visual perception.

Triangular pencils are a great innovation for aiding the adoption of correct 'straight grip' and, since this is the approved grip for writing, the companies that make them have made a great deal of money. They are useful for providing support for children with slower muscle development to be able to produce neater handwriting. However, what began as a useful tool for children with specific educational needs has, in some schools, become blanket provision, whether appropriate or not. Triangular pencils are far less convenient for children who are developing a 'right-angled wrist grip' and will make such children's handwriting worse. Left-handed 'right-angled wrist grip' children will be seriously disadvantaged. Triangular pencils are no good at all for drawing. It is hard, if not impossible, to hold them in either drawing position. Triangular *coloured* pencils are an anathema. They are impossible to use for shading.

The 'shading' grip (Figure 1.4) involves holding the instrument (pencil, pastel, and so on) horizontally in the palm-down hand, held between thumb and all four fingers. This is frequently also the sketching grip of choice for proficient adults with a strong visual sense as it is the most comfortable and fluid way to hold a pencil for drawing on a horizontal surface. The fingers are spread along the length of the instrument with the forefinger close to the tip for extra control. The thumb can move along the length of the instrument to fine-tune the balance and degree of

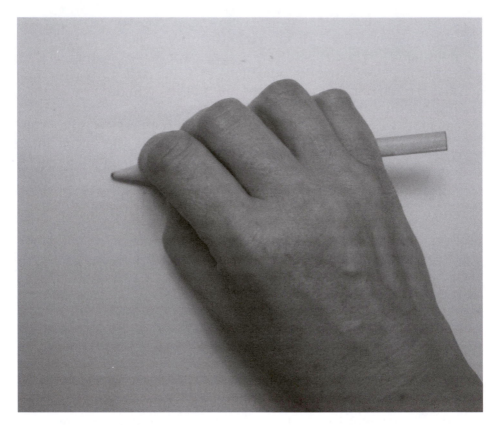

Figure 1.4   Shading grip

movement as required. Children should be taught to lay the pencil on its side for shading, which is the proper technique. Round coloured pencils are best for shading: they can be rolled in the fingers easily to keep the wear on the point even. Traditionally, school writing pencils were hexagonal to aid grip and colouring pencils were round to assist shading.

The 'correct' position for holding a drawing instrument (pencil, pen, charcoal, pastel, and so on), as taught to adults in traditional art classes, was for the instrument to be held in the whole hand pointing forward in a straight line from the elbow, through the wrist to the tip of the drawing instrument onto a vertical surface supported on an easel, as if the instrument was an extension of the pointing hand (Figure 1.5). This 'pointing' drawing grip was designed for standing at an easel and tracing onto paper the observed shapes of scenes and objects by moving the whole arm without moving the fingers. The artist needed only to check with a quick glance that they were getting the parts correctly placed on the paper and joined to each other. This skill was often taught by having students make observational drawings of very simple objects over

Figure 1.5   Pointing grip

and over again on the same, very large piece of paper. Apparently, examining Turner's landscape sketches reveal just how far he could draw between glances at the paper. The ability to coordinate the position of the hand on the paper with the position of objects in the observed scene could be taught to children in middle childhood as it once was, but the teaching of drawing technique went out of fashion about a hundred years ago because of the regimented way in which it was taught.

Adults who draw a lot will often change hand position according to felt need, adopting the 'straight grip', 'drawing grip' and 'right-angled wrist grip' at different times, even within one drawing, and will adopt different grips for different drawing tools. Unfortunately, only the writing grip is usually taught to young children in school. The usefulness of other grips for drawing are not demonstrated. Teachers should encourage children to try a range of grips for different purposes in order to extend their skill and capabilities in graphic expression.

Exploring materials and techniques

In the rest of this book, in discussion of the other dimensions of drawing, specific practical suggestions about materials and equipment are less frequently made, since the focus is on the way in which drawing can develop thinking and learning across the breadth of the curriculum. The following extended discussion on materials and techniques, therefore, should be held in mind and read into the use of the generic term 'drawing' throughout the remaining chapters of the book.

A range of drawing and mark-making materials should be available for children's use at all times. Early years teachers are usually better at this than those who teach older children. For some perverse reason, the older the children, the less choice they are offered, either of materials or techniques. It seems to be the view that little children need to experiment and older children need to be told what the limitations are. This seems counter-intuitive because little ones cannot learn everything at once and older ones have the maturity and experience to make informed choices. Paradoxically, therefore, the youngest children, with limited manual skills, experience and understanding can choose to draw or paint what they like with little teaching of techniques or discussion of how to approach the problem of expressing their viewpoint effectively. Yet at the top end of the primary school, children with much greater manual dexterity, knowledge of materials, techniques and greater personal awareness that enables them to reflect on experience in a variety of ways, are frequently given a tight brief and a limited range of materials with which to respond to it. Free choice time is rare in Key Stage 2 classrooms; free art time almost unheard of.

Even more paradoxical is the fear that teachers of older children sometimes seem to have of the mess that their class will make if given free rein, yet this seems to be containable by the organization within the average early years setting. Waste of resources is also frequently cited as a reason not to allow children free choice, yet the Early Years Foundation Stage Curriculum recognizes child-initiated learning as vital for children's social, intellectual and creative development. At all stages in the primary school it is important that techniques are taught and stimuli provided, but it is also vital that children are given time and space to explore on their own.

In all primary classrooms, therefore, children should be provided with and encouraged to use:

Fingers	And other parts of the body, including toes
Pencils	Full range from H to 6B, of as many thicknesses as possible
Felt pens	All thicknesses from flip chart pens to thin line markers
Ink pens	Ball pens, fibre tipped pens, fluid ink pens (Years 5–6)
Brushes	Thin sable ones are best for drawing. Try Chinese writing brushes too
Paint	In a range of types, colours, tones, textures, to use with a variety of implements
Charcoal	In stick form and as charcoal pencils
Graphite sticks	Really chunky as well as thin ones
Wax crayons	Out of fashion, need revival – thick and thin ones
Chalk and pastel	Use in conjunction with charcoal, not pencil
Sticks	Dip in different sorts of paint and ink
Tightly rolled paper	Try range of papers. Roll tightly and secure with sticky tape and dip in ink or paint. Fringe ends first if you like
Found objects	Anything that can be used to make a mark
Rubbers	Why not? Adults do. It is a sign of developing self-awareness, evaluative skills and desire to get things right. Only infants do not want rubbers.

Using *fingers* for painting either really appeals to 4–5-year-olds or they are repelled by getting their hands messy. The idea that all children should begin their experience of art in primary school with finger paints, although sounding logical, is not really valid. Many children will already have had experience of paintbrushes in nursery or at home and so may feel insulted and that they are going backwards in their artistic development. Teachers may need to provide a convincingly real context for using finger paints, such as using them on a non-absorbent surface in order to take prints. The thick consistency of commercial finger paints is ideal for this. However, making their own finger paint is exciting and trying it out can be an exploration and discussion of texture, viscosity and the effect of the angle at which the painting surface is held. Mixing powder paint with cornflour, glue powder, porridge oats, salt, sand and other common granular substances, then adding carefully controlled amounts of water can occupy children's interest in mixing, experimenting and mark-making, which may not yield any artistic products but will have contributed a great deal to children's understanding of material properties and mathematical proportions. It will also have stimulated language development, especially of adjectives to describe the gloopiness of the paints.

Even quite young children should experience a range of *pencils* from H to at least 4B and it is essential that children in upper Key Stage 2 are able to use an even wider range. It is impossible to learn to draw properly if only HB writing pencils are provided. Many artists use a 4B or even softer pencil for initial sketching. These soft pencils allow the image to be developed and modified without the need for a rubber, and Year 6 children should certainly be encouraged to rough out the outline and then gradually build the final image through overdrawing with a slightly harder pencil.

Felt pens and markers, ball pens and fibre tipped pens are popular with children as they give instant clear colour. Children frequently draw directly with these instruments, especially for their own pleasure, and then are dissatisfied with the results. In Key Stage 2, therefore, children can be shown that these implements should, for best results, be used to finally overdraw lines made by a soft pencil. Older children (Years 5 and 6) can experiment with pens that have more fluid ink (fountain pens and dip pens) but, again, greatest success in the final product is to be had when the ink is used to overdraw a pencilled line, although children need time to experiment and perfect their technique before limiting them to such overdrawing.

Thin *brushes* are best for drawing. Thick ones are for infilling a large area. The best brushes for drawing have flexible, soft bristles which come to a good point and can take up a decent quantity of paint or ink. Stiff hog's hair brushes produce poor lines and these are fine for the youngest experimenters with paint, but not for children in Key Stage 2. Chinese writing brushes work well with ink; they are designed for special block ink which is not expensive in China but may be difficult to obtain locally in many areas of the UK. These brushes are designed to be held upright, perpendicular to the paper laid on the table. Even if the correct brushes and ink cannot be obtained, children can use ordinary paint and sable brushes to experiment with the technique for holding the brush and try writing Chinese characters and creating Chinese pictures. The upright grip of the brush and the easy flow of the ink encourages a flowing style that is unique and enjoyable.

The problem with the *paints* that are available in most primary schools is that they frequently do not encourage techniques other than infilling drawings. The combination of cheap water-based paint (whether in powder, block or ready-mixed squeezy bottle) and grey sugar paper will hardly fire the imagination or develop a love affair with riotous colour. These water-based paints can be mixed with all manner of thickeners of different textures for children to experiment with possibilities. Mixing paint with PVA glue plus sand, lentils, oats, and so on, gives interesting textured effects that children can exploit to great visual effect by combining them with their knowledge of colour and form.

Charcoal and graphite sticks are messy but adaptable media in which to work. The blackness of the line varies with pressure and the stick breaks easily under too much pressure. Once children reach the stage of wanting to draw before painting, then charcoal is probably the best medium. They can be shown how to make both light and dark marks on the paper and need to be given time to experiment and come to understand the general rule of light marks for painting over and heavy marks for not.

Chalk and pastel can be used either on their own or in conjunction with charcoal and graphic sticks. All these materials have the same soft tonal qualities that can be shaded and merged into each other with the fingers. Looking at the pastel work of Degas or Monet demonstrates the versatility of the medium.

Teachers often confine the use of *wax crayons* to younger children. Years ago, large plastic tubs of grimy thick wax crayons with blunt ends were to be found in every primary classroom. From time to time new wax crayons would be bought and a new tub of grimy stubs produced, leaving the old one to fill a far corner of the cupboard. When the new crayons were in the same state as the old ones, the two would be mixed together and the sad process repeated. The advent of cheap felt pens largely saw the grateful demise of the grimy wax. If the wax crayons had been stored properly in single colour boxes, their ends kept sharpened and the children had been taught how to use them, then their demise would not have been so complete. Like charcoal, graphite, chalk and pastel, the quality of the mark depends on the pressure exerted. Also, like these other stick media, wax crayons can be used on their sides as well as in 'shading' and 'drawing' grip. Applied lightly, they can sketch an outline that can be overdrawn and infilled with heavier shading. With care, the shading can be faded out by beginning with hard pressure and lightening, or in reverse, beginning light and applying heavier pressure. These are techniques for confident capable hands in upper Key Stage 2 and it is worth reintroducing the thick wax crayons in Year 5 after the other stick media have been used. Making large sweeping lines with the side of a short crayon can give almost lyrical effects. Children should be encouraged to experiment with holding two crayons (or any other stick medium) together to make lines across large sheets of paper. This playing with materials and lines can help older children feel the early joy in the act of mark-making that they experienced as infants and of which their more recent concerns for pictorial accuracy has robbed them.

This is also true of drawing with *sticks, tightly rolled paper* and *other found objects* dipped in paint of various consistencies and textures, as described above. Making and experimenting with mark-making tools provide opportunities to develop hand skills and visual vocabulary away from the need to produce an accurate likeness of anything. Children may, as a result, decide to try to draw something, probably a well-practised image, with a newly created tool to see how it works. They are unlikely to produce an innovative image at the same time as playing with and learning to wield something unfamiliar, except by serendipity. Creativity requires knowledge of the technique and the materials for its expression and so learning to use new materials differently is not likely to produce the children's greatest pieces of art. However, it allows them to be less concerned about the image as they focus on the effects of the tools, the lines they produce, the amount and type of paint that works well, and so on. In order to allow reflection and later build on the experience, the children need to annotate their experiments, to record the tool and paint type used on each sample. This can then become an almost scientific quest, with the annotation aiding the evaluation and comparison of different tools. This new knowledge can then be applied in a new context, perhaps in combination with collage materials to make a composite picture or abstract work.

Playing with ideas

The ability to use drawing as a powerful means of playing with ideas, exploring themes, expressing feeling and reactions, and of communicating these to others, is heavily dependent on the child's confidence and capability with a range of drawing media and techniques. As well as encouraging children to experiment with a range of drawing media, the use of drawing for drafting needs also to be encouraged. Drafting is a way of playing with ideas that can be evaluated, discussed and advice sought before final commitment, often in another media.

At age 5, children will draw an outline shape in paint and then fill it in but they soon choose to draw in lead pencil and then colour in the shapes. They have realized that the lead pencil gives them the freedom to rub out and change parts of the drawing with which they are dissatisfied. By Year 3 this pencil line drawing often includes the kinds of small details that would be best left undrawn and put in after the paint has dried. By Year 5 (age 9–10 years) children should be encouraged to develop the process of making a painting through creating several layers, using techniques such as applying light background washes before drawing the foreground details.

This applies equally to children's approach to other genres, such as collage where time and effort is wasted on drawing to an inappropriate level of detail or on unnecessarily correcting details of the drawing, where it would be more sensible to cover the whole background first, or even simply draw a plan on scrap paper and use it as a guide without drawing onto the background at all. Lower Key Stage 2 children, especially, often make quite detailed drawings onto backing paper, only to cover these over with large collage pieces, thereby obliterating the only record of what they have spent so long working out. Perhaps this may be because they have been involved in group activities in early years or Key Stage 1 classrooms in which an adult provides a large drawing to which children glue scrunched up tissue paper or small pieces of collage materials to make a mosaic. The children, naturally, believe that this is a technique they are meant to follow in every circumstance.

Plentiful and generous opportunities should be given for children to invent and try out their own ideas, but as Maureen Cox comments: 'sooner or later most of us will actually require tuition in order to give substance to our ideas; without it we will lose interest, thus insuring no improvement, no self-expression and no creativity' (1992: 7). In the early years of life, children manage to pick up a good deal with little or no formal tuition, but later on their own standards of what constitutes a good drawing far outstrips their skills. Without tuition, says Cox, most people cannot draw, and so lose interest and give up altogether. The ability to draw is not natural or automatic, there are skills to acquire and practise. Unlike many writers on children's drawings, Cox is happy with children copying, since many adult artists do this to improve their skill. She is also happy with cartoons (in contrast to some other writers) as this denotes a widening of children's repertoire and increases their manual control of drawing instruments and self-confidence.

Those writers who approach drawing purely as an 'art' activity seem frequently to want to limit the repertoire of acceptability, as if wanting to train children into the kind of drawings that they see as part of the canon of 'art' and exclude by omission all the many other uses of drawing which children may use, enjoy and exploit. This delineation into art/non-art, permitted/not-permitted puts restrictions on the activity, imposes artificial boundaries and prevents the child from seeing that this very powerful medium for generating and expressing ideas can be used to advantage to model and convey ideas including, but also beyond, those of art. Limiting the child's output to a small range of accepted types generates insecurity. The child 'cannot draw' because they feel they cannot produce the kind of images that are acceptable to the teacher and in front of their peers. If opportunities were provided to develop a far greater graphic range, then children would feel less inhibited.

To identify and discuss some of the dimensions of that graphic range is the aim of this book. Drawing is constantly and uninhibitedly used by adults: from sketch maps to show directions, to quick sketches of room layouts with dimensions to work out how many floor tiles are needed, to family trees, to instructions of how to put flat-pack cupboards together, and so on. Adults rarely make apologies for their lack of artistic finesse when they do these sketches. They are using drawing to think, to plan, to communicate where words fail or are inappropriate. Children need to be shown examples of these and teachers should collect them from their friends and relatives. Accurate observational drawing is just one genre within the field. It is also the one in which playing with ideas through drawing is, for the child at least, the least likely to happen.

Drawing is a powerful means of playing with ideas across a broad field of endeavour, and this is the message of this book. Some thinkers would want to include writing within drawing and there are powerful arguments to support this view. However, that approach is not taken in this book, although writing and graphics frequently interact (and are consciously used interactively) in playing with ideas and this should be encouraged where appropriate. There are occasions when writing is more appropriate than drawing (a list of possibilities, for instance) and labelling of drawings frequently enables clarification, and acts as a prop for understanding ambiguity or plain poor drawing. Children are frequently happy to use drawing for generating design ideas once they realize that verbal labels are possible and accepted. The recording of ideas as they occur and the mind moves on to the next possibility needs to be quick and useful.

Looking at sheets of paper that have been used by adults for idea generation will reveal a mess of ideas, some written, some drawn, overwritten, overdrawn, arrows and squiggles, underlying and crossing out (and even crossings out crossed out). This interactivity, the conversation with the drawing, is the zenith of using the *process* of drawing as a means of playing with ideas. The ideas are coming faster and the connections with other good ideas are being realized almost faster than the human mind can compute them. Making the marks that cement one idea can stop the next idea in its tracks. Speed of recording, by whatever means, is of the essence and marking the relationships between new thought and past thought is a dynamic process that can continue at full tilt and with total absorption until the thought wave is exhausted and the need to sit back and review comes. Then comes the process of reorganization of the thoughts and ideas, which will prompt redrafting in a more readable format. New lines of enquiry can be suggested in this reorganization as the mind takes on a more systematic review of the multitude of ideas that intertwine and litter the page.

Children can do this. They do it spontaneously before they become aware of picture-making and of social expectations that their drawings will be pictorial. They also do it at the stage of emergent writing, when they use drawing and writing interactively to place-mark their story ideas as they record the ongoing narrative that they are creating. This skill can be extended and developed throughout the primary years by encouraging children to use drawing for designing, to use drawing and writing interactively to record observations in scientific enquiries, to brainstorm in groups about a topic for class debate or to support, develop and explain their mathematical reasoning.

One of the inhibitors to the realization of this potential within children's work is their need and desire to master the mechanics. Developing neat writing is frequently more important to the child than recording a creative storyline. Drawing something accurately and realistically is more important to them than roughly indicating its existence. Anning (1993) recorded how her colleagues' use of the words 'scribbling down some ideas' produced horrified reactions from the 6-year-olds with whom they were working. 'Scribbling' was for babies; they drew properly. More than this, their aspiration was to draw ever more properly.

Summary

The booklet 'Start Drawing' produced by the Campaign for Drawing (2002), categorizes the use of drawing as being for perception, communication and manipulation. The authors speak of the way in which young children will develop one theme or image across many drawings but this could equally be applied to the work of the greatest adult artists, scientists, designers or thinkers who use graphic means to generate, develop, organise and play with ideas:

'reflexive oscillation' between impulse, ideas and mark, receiving feedback from the marks appearing on the page, which prompt further thought and mark-making. Usually the drawing is one of a series, where ideas are explored, repeated, refined, practised, worked over, discarded, combined, where alternatives are sought and alternative possibilities explored. (Campaign for Drawing, 2002: 2)

This encapsulates the use of drawing for playing with ideas, the inter-play between product and process, Container and Journey. It is close to the ideal practice of using drawing to design, the title of the sixth dimension discussed in this book. Between early playing with materials and techniques and a lifetime's experimentation in using drawing for developing powerful innovative ideas lies informed knowledge and capability in a universal and multifaceted tool for human creativity. Inherent in that facility are the layers of meanings ascribed to the lines, dots and squiggles, to their ambiguities as well as to their clarity. The second dimension, 'Drawing to mean', focuses on this all-important aspect of drawing, which, like 'Drawing to play', continues to flow as an under-current through the other dimensions until explicitly recombining in 'Drawing to design'.

Dimension 2

Drawing to mean

(Children) draw before they can write, and they associate their drawings with thought even before they can draw anything recognizable. (Silver, 1978: 51)

As discussed in 'Dimension 1: Drawing to play', the urge to experiment and to create new forms seems to be a human imperative, almost an obsession. These forms frequently contain and convey meaning, even when apparently completely abstract, and viewers often seek recognizable forms in abstract art, such as the patterns that Jackson Pollock produced by trails of paint from swinging tins. Abstract art depends for its emotional impact on the meaning that we attach to basic shapes, patterns and colours, and large canvases of a single colour are frequently interpreted according to the cultural significance of that colour. For instance, white might convey calm, cold or death to three different viewers from different cultural traditions.

Humans build new concepts, understandings and meanings by extrapolation from what is already known, which includes the ability to recognize and exploit the metaphors and symbolism of their home culture. The human capability to be creative stems from the human mind's capacity for playful invention and metaphorical insight, which have led to the greatest achievements of the human species: the creation of the emotionally charged symbolic systems of literature, music and art. The meanings conveyed in all three forms are multifaceted, overlaid as well as underpinned by cultural meanings and emotional subtlety. This seems to have been so from the earliest days of evolution of Homo sapiens, and may have been one of the distinguishing traits that separated us from our sister species:

The progress of the human mind, when considered genetically, is seen to consist, not as is commonly thought, merely of a number of accretions, added from without, but of the following two processes: on of the one hand the constant unmasking of previous symbolisms, the recognition that these, though previously thought to be literally true, were really only aspects of the truth, the only ones of which our minds were – for either affective or intellectual reasons – at the time capable. (Jones, 1962: 30)

This is a fascinating assertion, which, in asserting the primacy of symbolism over realism, would seem to go against intuition, whether thinking of the development of the individual or the whole human species. However, the meaning which infants attach to early drawings seem to suggest a symbolic rather than a realistic intent. There appears to be a human urge to make one thing represent another which occurs so early in life that it seems more likely to be genetic than learnt behaviour. As creators of visual imagery, both children and adults are actively seeking, creating and adapting already existing symbolic forms in which to convey ever deeper layers of meaning. The relationships between form and content, sign and meaning, metaphor, analogy and symbolism, are the interwoven threads of the discussion of 'Drawing to mean'.

Creating meaning

This concept of the active involvement (the term 'enactive' is frequently used) of the person in creating their personal perception of the external world through interaction between feeling, seeing and reasoning, asserted by Piaget, Vygotsky and Bruner, is supported by recent developments in neuro-science research. The term 'enaction' suggests creation, agency and purposeful self-motivated enquiry. It involves process thinking: thinking *within* a system, yet also *with* or *through* the system. In drawing, this involves thinking about the form and the development of the drawing itself, while thinking about the content and the meaning that is being conveyed as the drawing develops substance and form, in other words, the purposeful creation of the container for ideas on a journey.

Goldschmidt (1994: 162) called this interaction the '*fabrication* of visual displays' (original italics), putting the process of drawing in a place of power in the creation of meaning. She makes reference to Wittgenstein's (1969) concept of *imaging as doing* rather than receiving. This sense of active creation of visual image to actively generate and develop thought, rather than simply record what is seen, as a camera or automata might do, is fundamental to the use of drawing in whatever context of human endeavour, whether for art, design, science or mathematics. The human usage is to create meaning, not simply to record. Perception, and even observation, is mediated through the human brain, and meaning is determined and conveyed through the drawn forms.

At any age, whether as a child, a young person or an adult, as soon as someone has developed sufficient mastery over a technique or in a particular media, they will use it to *say* something. Creating, establishing, developing and communicating *meaning* becomes the reason for drawing, whether this be via a personal, idiosyncratic statement or using well-established, culturally semiotic and symbolic forms. As infants develop their ability to process their perceptions and observations of the world around them, so they begin also to look for ways in which they can communicate their thoughts and ideas visually as well as through language. They learn gestures (waving bye-bye) as well as the words that go with them. It is not surprising, therefore, that they expect gestures that leave marks (drawing) to hold and communicate meaning too.

There has been considerable debate over the status of drawing as visual language, with those who regularly use visual representation to generate and communicate ideas (artists, designers) claiming that it is, and, predictably, others claiming equally strongly that it is not. The arguments hinge on the definition of language. If a language is seen as a method of communication to convey meaning, using established conventions and which is comprehensible to others, then drawing falls into the field of language. If, however, language requires syntax and semantics, the formal elements of grammar, then only speech and writing can really be classified as language, with musical, scientific and mathematical notation falling into the grey zone. However, the increased use of graphic symbols, icons and signage, whether on the computer desktop, as function indicators on electronic equipment, traffic signs, trademarks and so on, means that we 'read' an increasing number of graphic symbols as if they were words. For simple labelling the modern world is moving to the position achieved by China's first emperor hundreds of years ago: decide on a system of universal graphic symbols that remain standard regardless of the spoken languages of the people.

The problem with the debate is the underlying assumptions of hierarchy within communication systems, with those viewed as most cerebral and abstract (writing, mathematics) at the top of the tree and all other systems trying to scramble up the branches and justify their place by trying to describe what they do in the terms that are more appropriate to other systems. Thus, in order to justify the claims that drawing is linguistic, terms such as 'the grammar of drawing' have been invented, but this fails to move the argument forward as it cannot be decided what this grammar might consist of. Furthermore, 'grammar' implies rules that everyone agrees to conform to and use in communication with each other. People who use drawing powerfully frequently bend and break rules just as, in reality, creative speakers and writers do.

The better questions, therefore, are: does drawing speak? Does a drawing communicate? Does it contain and convey meaning? Does it use a symbolic system to generate, develop and reflect upon observations of the physical, social, emotional and abstract worlds? Since drawing can do all of these things, then it would seem that drawing has many of the qualities of a linguistic system (Aritzpe and Styles, 2003). Visual meaning, however, does not always translate well into words, depending as it does on colour, form, shapes and tone: 'There are values and meanings that can be expressed only by immediate visible and audible qualities, and to ask what they mean in the sense of something that can be put into words is to deny their distinctive existence' (Dewey, 1978: 74). Viewing all systems of communication as equal but different is probably a more helpful approach to the debate. That drawing does so differently from speech, writing or mathematics does not mean that drawing is a second-class form of language, but that it is a different form of communication that says different things in different ways, some of which it does more effectively and efficiently than other communicative systems:

For instance:

- A picture can often convey what words cannot say.
- A map shows the way where words would be so complicated that getting lost would be guaranteed.
- A diagram shows the relationship of parts to each other, spatially or conceptually.
- A design sheet shows possibilities from which a customer can choose the option they believe best fits their needs.
- An icon stimulates worship and confirms faith.
- A portrait, a landscape or a battle scene may have a subtext that can be read just as surely as the subtext in a work of literature.

And so we could go on, listing the many uses of drawing to create and convey meaning in a host of contexts across history and cultures, and which children begin to use as soon as they begin to impute meaning to their own symbolic actions. Although talking primarily about spoken and written language, Wells's (1986) description of children as 'Meaning Makers' is equally applicable to their explorations and exploitations of visual form.

In addition, the meaning of the drawing process for the child may well be very different from the meaning attached to the drawn product through the eyes of an observing adult. Children are not just creators of meaning, but subverters too, using the context of adult-initiated activities for their own ends. This includes their social agenda, and the activity of drawing being used for creating and maintaining social bonds, stability and group dynamics, and even of power relationships between group members.

Metaphor and analogy

The central metaphors for drawing (Container and Journey) used in this book, are drawn from Lakoff and Johnson's (1980) book *Metaphors We Live By*, whose central tenet is that humans build new knowledge through perceiving metaphorical connections within the new situation or problem with knowledge and understanding that they already possess. Lakoff and Johnson's word 'metaphor' assumes within it such related words as analogy, metonym and extrapolation. On this view, the ability to use drawing to enable thinking hinges on seeing the potential for drawing to act as an analogical bridge between the real world of observation, the inner world of the imagination, and the realm of conscious seeing, thinking and feeling. There is also a metonymic sense here, as the content of a drawing is viewed, discussed and developed as if it were the real object. For instance, in a Year 4 class, a roughly sketched fastener on a bag was the focus of an animated discussion. Two girls were waving their hands in the air, miming how it might work, how it might be attached, how easy it would be to open and close one-handed when the bag was hanging over the shoulder. The simple line drawing, representing only half-formed ideas, was being discussed as if it were already the object it suggested.

A series of drawings can represent a stream of ideas, each springing from the last, as multiple possibilities for a design, multiple extrapolations from the original thought. This becomes most apparent when drawing is used in a design context. Key Stage 2 children will look at each other's drawings and make comments about how something might work, how it might be improved or even suggest other possibilities. Drawing can become a discussion document between a group of children, each using drawing to image possibilities and sketch ideas to communicate to others in the group what they might do together. This ability to extrapolate from the drawn form into a possible future construction depends on the ability to perceive and manipulate visual analogies between the idea in the mind's eye and its drawn form, and to project both into an imagined future existence. The ability to share these mind's eye views with others through drawing depends on the shared capability to read drawings symbolically, not necessarily on the drawing's realistic likeness to any object that exists in the real world. This is equally true of rough sketches for art as for relational diagrams for mathematical or conceptual mapping.

Whatever area of human knowledge is being represented, new meaning is constructed from meanings that we already hold, frequently by perceiving similarity or analogy, by extrapolation or exploiting metaphor. Although Pye (1964) is primarily talking about adults, the following comments apply equally to children's inventiveness: 'Invention can only be done deliberately if the inventor can discern similarities between the particular result which he is envisaging and some other results which he has seen and stored in his memory … An inventor's power to invent depends on his ability to see analogies between results …' (Pye, 1964: 27).

From babyhood, children build their knowledge and understanding of the world through their ability to see similarities and analogies between the form of one object or event and another, to build up a picture of how the world is organized, how information is classified and how the social world functions. This skill is fundamental to using drawing, as it is to any representational system. Arnheim (1969) concluded that analogical perception is basic to intelligent behaviour and that our inherent topological skills, which enable similarities and analogies to be perceived, are what make productive thinking possible. The ability to see analogy is essential when problem-solving, as well as in successful transfer of learning through overcoming contextual barriers, perhaps by focusing attention on the abstract character of potential solutions (Gick and Holyoak, 1985).

The ability to use analogy is dependent on the ability to create an inner representation, or model, of the problem and match potential solutions to this inner model. Objectification of both problem and potential solutions, for example, through drawing, makes these visible and more readily evaluated. Gentner (1982) called these models 'structure mappings' from one domain of human knowledge or experience to another. In researching the role of analogy in the development of scientific concepts, she compared scientific 'explanatory analogies' to 'expressive analogies', which are the province of the semanticist. There is also, however, an additional class of 'exploratory analogies' which are not discussed by Gentner and which are used to play with ideas, and which would also, perhaps, include allegory and paracosm and even daydreaming.

Drawing can support all three of these forms of analogical thinking, since it is a kind of 'parallel system' (Tourangeau, 1982: 25) that supports analogical thinking through being one itself. Working within a parallel system, in Tourangeau's sense, is the process of being able to think completely in one system, such as drawing, and come to logical conclusions about a parallel target system (for example, creating multiple forms of racing cars across a series of drawings, drawing a sketch map to show someone how to find their way to your house, making an accurate drawing of an important archaeological find). The ability to create and think completely within a system and come to logical conclusions within it, while fully aware that it is a created system which parallels another, seems common to both fantasy role play and the creative use of drawing. Whether using drawing to create and record new ideas and insights, or playing out a role in an imaginary world, people can think within the confines of a system, manipulate it and make logical domain-appropriate decisions within it, in juxtaposition with a domain-parallel system and mentally switching back and forth from one to the other. This manipulation of mental schema does not seem far from the understanding of allegory or the construction of paracosms. It seems, therefore, likely that children who can create whole fantasy worlds in their head are generally better at creative activities and possibly use drawing more innovatively than their less imaginative peers.

To create and explore meaning through drawing requires an immersion in the process, to think in it, manipulate it, make parallels and juxtapositions and jump back and forth from inner and outer reality using the drawing as place-holder for ideas, while brokering possibilities. Drawing acts as an intermediary between this ability to transfer between the inner and outer reality and enables the construction of meaning. It is a powerful creative tool, a medium for making inner thoughts and perceptions externally manifest and available for reflection and scrutiny.

Wittgenstein (1969) called this ability 'seeing as', which implies active engagement with metaphoric meanings. Drawing can have a metonymic function, in which the drawing is viewed as if it is the real object. Looking at illustrations in a car manual, for instance, enables understanding of where a particular part is situated, how it is removed, taken apart, mended and refitted. To take a more abstract example, geometrical figures are read as if they represented the properties of the real world, although such perfect shapes rarely, if ever, exist in nature. Such drawings are seen as if they represent the real shapes and configurations of things. A different sort of 'seeing as' operates in the world of art. Drawings may convey emotions or moods or even be designed to enhance spiritual perceptions. In these instances, the 'seeing as' has an almost allegorical sense.

Across the metaphorical range of uses of drawing, the same processes are operating: inner image within the brain is projected onto an external surface, such that the lines created are 'seen as if' they were the real object being designed, the specific memory being clarified, the perception being recorded or the imagination running riot. By pinning down fleeting thoughts and ideas, recording them for future review and consideration, drawing acts as container for possibilities on a journey of exploration. The juxtaposition of two conflicting or complementary ideas may create new meanings, intentionally, serendipitously or as a playful 'let's see' that develops into fruitful possibilities. The analogical use of drawing

Figure 2.1   Andy's map

includes abstract systems of representation such as many of the relational diagrams used for modelling mathematical and scientific ideas.
This would include the kinds of diagrams used in graph theory to
analyse and portray complex systems (see 'Dimension 4: Drawing to
know'). A familiar example is the London Underground map, which
represents the nodes (the stations) but not the distances between them,
the links are straight lines (unlike the real tracks) and even the directions are approximate, the clarity of the layout having taken priority
over realistic representation. Outterside (1993) made an interesting
claim, that children's first named graphic products are often analogues:
they look nothing like what they represent, although they have meaning assigned to them by the child. This might even suggest, perhaps,
that children who produce many such drawings would possibly become
more adept at using drawing for modelling ideas than those who see
drawing as a more static representation of observations.

Figure 2.1 was produced by a boy called Andy at 4 years old, who
had a delayed speech problem, soon after his entry to nursery class.

He was asked to draw a picture about what he had done at the weekend and when asked by the teacher to 'Tell me about your picture' he said 'the beach' and 'brother'. It was kept in his 'Baseline entry folder' and given back to him to take home some 18 months later. He became very excited at the sight of it and recounted the day on the beach and pointed out what the various parts of the drawing represented. He said:

> It's a map. We went on a boat on it. There's big waves, like that big. I saw people writing with fingers on sand, saying 'Liam' – and that (pointing to writing on right). And a boat nearly sank. And then we did, got fishing out. We got some worms and we catched some fish and got our fishing rods and put them in the sea and we fished.

There are two noteworthy aspects to this episode: first, that he could read it so long afterwards, when he was still unable to read many written words; second, that he called it a map. To an adult it looks like so much scribble, but his reading of it gives the drawing total sense. Andy demonstrates an awareness of what a map is, as a graphic representation of a route. His drawing indicates the use of line to indicate both time and space. He is inventing his own way of representing the event, based on his ability to move lines around the page, enjoying the blue that represents the sea and using it to colour in the shapes that have been made by his lines. He appears then to have become interested in the formal construction of the picture he is making on the page. The blue colouring is fitted neatly into the shapes the lines have made. He uses a spiral motion to good effect to differentiate a space within other spaces. He makes his colouring lines in different directions, experimenting in the aesthetic effects of shading.

Andy was far more interested in content and lacked the knowledge of semiotic conventions of form that would make his drawing understandable to others. Without his explanation, it had been dismissed as a scribble. He was, however, actively experimenting with an abstract representation form of a quite sophisticated kind. Unfortunately for Andy, the children who had already concentrated on semiotic form and developed a range of less fluid but more conventional symbols for their ideas were probably receiving greater praise from the Nursery staff. Ironically, his drawing was preserved only because it was seen as an example of his delayed development. His poor speech at the time prevented him from conveying its meaning but even if he had been able to explain it, it is unlikely that it would have been highly valued, since iconic capability is the drawing skill most frequently praised and encouraged in Nursery and Reception class settings.

Semiotics and symbolism

Semiotics, the study of signs that convey meaning, includes the analysis of features of visual communication (foreground/background, left/right, engagement/opposition, and so on) as well as the placement and interaction of these features with each other and with textual and other symbolic content. The ability to read signs is a universal human capability. The human brain is geared to perceive topological features which 'inform the organism of the typical character of things' (Arnheim, 1969: 77). Biologically, this probably springs from the ability of all creatures to respond appropriately to the minimum necessary relevant features in their landscape. Knowing which signs matter and what they mean develops to a degree commensurate with the environmental and social complexity of the species' lifestyle, which for humans means that cultural signs have become increasingly important and increasingly dependent on the symbolism of language: spoken, written and graphic.

Recognizing these signs, and learning to use them, is one of the most important jobs of childhood. Within every human society on Earth, learning the semiotic reference set is an important social as well as cognitive skill, whether these are gestural, linguistic, musical or graphic. The ability to recognize, correctly interpret and use these signs for effective communication is an essential part of growing up into a useful and full member of that society. Human social signs, however, are not just manipulative in the way that gestures and vocalizations are used by other species. The semiotic set of human interaction includes symbolism, which is actively produced from a surprisingly young age.

When an infant looks at their action with a pencil and declares 'This is Mummy', they have demonstrated an awareness of the symbolic function of drawn images. What they have produced on the paper will look nothing like 'Mummy', it is probably a circular or cross-hatched scribble, but the leap of the child's imagination has transformed it into 'Mummy'. What is remarkable about this mental leap is that they have not produced something that anyone else could recognize as 'Mummy'. They have not been playing with a pencil, produced a recognizable human figure and sat back and thought 'That looks like my Mummy'. They have leapt straight in at the symbolic deep end without an awareness of semiotics.

There is a parallel here with the way in which speech develops. Athey (1990) refers to the work of Stern (1924) in which scribbling and babbling were seen as parallels, and adds that babbling turns into talking through the interaction of adults with the infant and that most parents recognize that babblings have meanings. Babies begin by making a narrow range of multi-purpose sounds, for hunger, pain, fear, tiredness and so on. To tired parents, happy sounds seem to come as a second wave. Babies begin to recognize specific voices around them almost from birth, and specific sounds, such as their own name or referent ('babby' for instance) within their first few months. They begin to produce sounds that seem increasingly word-like and parents listen hard for the first truly accurate word-bite. From the baby's perspective, it must seem that they have been making meaningful sounds for a long time, so what is so special about this particular production? What is remarkable about naming drawings is that the urge to do so frequently comes from the child, without specific prolonged coaching from adults. In comparison to the way in which adults coo, smile and talk motherese to babies within moments of birth, no comparable early coaching in graphic production takes place much beyond providing infants with pen, paper and some encouragement.

Largely self-motivated, therefore, the infant makes and practices a range of marks on paper and, as their proficiency in mark-making develops, they can put intentionality into the performance, and naming of drawings may come spontaneously or in response to an adult's question. It is probably a false trail to try to distinguish whether or not an adult's input pushes the child into seeing the scribble as representing something. For some children, the adult may provide the stimulus for the great 'aha' moment, some may realize this for themselves and get re-enforcement of the idea later.

Observing this self-motivation might have underlain the belief of Kellogg (1959) that asking the child the meaning of their mark-making is not just irrelevant but likely to damage the biological development of art. However, as Athey (1990) and Matthews (2002) so rightly point out, more recent evidence has shown that children whose artwork is discussed with them develop much more confidence and show greater range and maturity in their artwork. Neither Kellogg (1959) nor Lowenfeld (1957) seemed to consider these desirable effects of the encouragement on which children thrive or the ensuing extension of children's capabilities through interaction with supportive and interested adults. The idea that adults should leave children alone to develop their drawings in their own way is in complete contrast to the way we think about every other skill that children will learn, from doing up buttons to learning to read. If a conversation with an infant puts them on the road to understanding such a major cognitive building block as visual symbolic representation, so much the better. The adult has taught the child something new and valuable. This should be celebrated, not denigrated.

Once the child's capability with a drawing instrument enables them to reliably repeat similar shapes and patterns on different occasions, then they will repeat these in various combinations for a range of purposes in order to represent what they know about the world around them. Playing with both form and content are important in the development of children's drawings. In practising the same form in many contexts, the child develops a symbol system that can be used to express a range of subjects. The semicircle may be a rainbow or a boat. The square becomes the house, the shop, the body of an animal, a lorry, and so on. Athey (1990) makes the point that both form and content of early drawings are important for understanding the nature of the development of children's drawings. He criticized Kellogg (1959) for paying no attention to content and Eng (1931) for discounting form, focusing purely on the range of different subjects that her daughter Margaret drew, without seeing in them the commonalities of form that the child was exploring.

Once a child has discovered a graphic symbol that is usefully recognizable and repeatable, it is not surprising that they use it over and over again until they become dissatisfied with its limitations for new purposes and want to abandon it for something new that they perceive to be better. The development of a good range of graphic forms makes representation of content easier and communication with others more effective. By about age 4 years, children have a range of such basic forms at their disposal. These usually include circles, straight lines (horizontal, vertical and diagonal), zigzags, arcs (including semicircles), dots and dashes, and free-form scribbles. They soon acquire the ability to draw squares and triangles with somewhat rounded corners. Angles are difficult, since these require the ability to precisely stop the pencil and move off in a different direction. Circles can be elongated into ellipses and sausage shapes, which can then be used for legs and arms. More complex shapes, such as hats, drawn as a single line develop in most children's sixth year, as do the abilities to imagine the shape of the human body and to draw a clothed figure without first needing to draw the limbs. Proportion suffers (hands and ears are especially large in comparison to the rest of the figure) but this is a trade-off against the greater complexity of form (Figure 2.2).

However, children are unlikely to be creating new forms and extending their range of content at the same time, and certainly not within the same drawing. Learning a new technique or mastering a new medium is all-consuming, even for adults, and being creative while learning something new is not possible. A sufficient level of mastery is required before new knowledge or skill can be used creatively. This

Figure 2.2   Human figure by Kayleigh, aged 4

applies to the development of graphic symbols as well as to physical capability.

For instance, Helena, aged 7, is drawing a family outside their house. What will she put in the sky? The rest of her friends are drawing blue sky and a sun, but she draws clouds with her pencil because all the blue pens are in use. There is a grey felt pen available so she colours the clouds grey. This has completely changed the look of the picture. She was going to draw flowers in the garden but does dashes of rain instead. It comes down on the girl in the picture. It makes Helena feel uncomfortable, as if sadness was raining down, which is not what she intended to convey. She looks across the table and sees one of the boys doing lightning zapping a baddy. She looks back at her own drawing, draws lightning coming from one cloud and then a rainbow from the other to the earth, filling the empty space on the right-hand side of her picture. Helena is now happy. She has created a new meaning through seeing the potential resolution to her dissatisfaction through appropriating the lightning imagery from a different context. She now has a picture that has a more subtle and sophisticated message than appears to be produced by her friends. Helena has not only created a satisfying resolution to her predicament but has a new visual device for representing the happy resolution of conflict and sadness. The rainbow is stored away in her mind for future occasions and will be repeated long after she has consciously forgotten the conflict of representation that it was employed to resolve.

Throughout their primary school years, children adapt and build on the basic symbolic forms established by the age of 7. Drawing complex shapes, including the human body, in one continuous line requires sufficient practice in drawing the component parts separately to be able to image them onto the surface and draw round them all in one line. This leads to interesting distortions during first attempts but is a skill much admired by other children once mastered. The child is constantly trying to develop form while conveying content, leading, almost inevitably, to dissatisfaction with form and a sense of frustration with the whole process, especially as they have to frequently juxtapose images from different registers. Thus a child may have a well-developed schema for representing a person, which they happily employ alongside other semiotic forms for houses, horses, and so on. The increasingly complex demands on their locational drawing skills (for example, draw Henry VIII sitting on his horse arriving outside Hampton Court) creates conflict between semiotics and perception of how things really look. The desire and attempt to abandon the semiotic form in order to create more realistic images occupies children across the years of middle childhood and beyond.

Bruner (1979) suggested three kinds of *representation of knowledge*:

- iconic – direct pictorial representation
- enactive – a picture indicating something that it is not actually a picture of, for example, smoke rising indicates presence of fire
- symbolic – non-pictorial graphic whose meaning is specific, for example, numeral, letter, arrow, tick.

Note: Bruner's use of the word 'enactive' is different to that used above in the discussion about creating meaning and is closer to the analogical drawings, discussed under 'Metaphor and analogy'.

This categorization should not be read hierarchically. It is not the case that pictorial representation, which the child from age 7 years onwards struggles increasingly to attain and which is actively encouraged by teachers, is the lowest level of knowledge representation in Bruner's thought. Representing an observation with whatever degree of realism requires complex cognitive processing, so this does not indicates a less complex knowledge about the object or situation. On the other hand, while symbolic representation may require high levels of abstract thought and metaphorical capability, the infant's symbol for 'Mummy' is closer to the abstract symbolism of writing or numerals than is the older child's careful rendering of a seashell with shading and texture.

From his reading of both Piaget's and Bruner's thinking, as well as from his own research, Athey (1990) concluded that there may be two different kinds of cognitive patterning, one evolving from *early action* and the other from *early perception*. However, he seems to assume that only cognitive development from early perception leads to figurative representation (including drawing), which is only true if drawing is seen as a way of recording perception rather than resulting from direct action. Children's earliest experiments with drawing instruments seem often to be more about exploring action than representing perceptions of the world. It is only once the child has realized the potential for pictorial representation by means of the marks that they are making that representation of perception can begin to take place. This is made possible by the infant's physical capability in wielding the mark-making instrument, but one child may be declaring wild scribbles to be 'Mummy' while another may be making neat precise lines that are produced for the sheer enjoyment of the process.

Drawing and writing

Vygotsky (1986) asserted that children's early drawing is a form of graphic speech, a precursor to written language. However, through pressure for children to become 'literate' in a very narrow definition of the term, adults may be tempted to move children on quickly from using drawing to develop stories into producing a neat written product as a final version that is less rich and less meaningful to the child and does little for their expressive and creative development. Traditionally, many teachers insisted that children write first and draw afterwards, to the detriment of the easy flow of ideas. It is not surprising that many children's writing is unimaginative if they have to repeatedly stop the flow of ideas in order to check spellings or concentrate on the correct formation of letters, not to mention worrying about where to place full stops, capital letters, commas and speech marks.

Combinations of pictures with text and text-like symbols are common among the output of 4–5-year-olds. Their experience of everyday environmental print, such as cereal packets, supermarket carrier bags, and other familiar food, entertainment and household items that often use a combination of text and graphics, provide ready models for this genre. At first, children do not distinguish between writing and graphic symbols; they communicate equally the nature of the product. Yet even by age 4 years, some children are aware of the difference between pictures, patterns and text, and are beginning to experiment with the production of written symbols, both separately and in conjunction with drawn images. The child may use letters of their name, numbers or other letters of the alphabet with which they are familiar, or even invent some of their own. They know that letters and words say things about a picture, having seen this convention repeatedly in use all around them. They are not yet sure which letters and words say what, or even the forms that letters take. However, by entry into Key Stage 1 at age 5 years, most children already possess the skill of combining graphics and text. At this early stage, there appears to be a reciprocal relationship between young children's drawings and writing. Harste et al. (1984) concluded that graphics and emergent writing skills combine and support each other. However, it can be the case that as children become more competent writers, drawing takes a secondary role, from which it is difficult to resurrect it.

Children's earliest attempts at recording narratives and conveying a story on paper frequently rely on the interactive use of drawing and written symbols (single letters, and so on) as a means of 'place-holding' (Hammond, 1997) The child can recall and recount the ideas which were flowing in their heads at the time, retelling a story based on these marks. At this emergent writing stage, young children use pictures and single letters, occasionally odd words, or even just marks and squiggles to place-hold their ideas. This ability to use drawing and text interactively to place-hold narrative is a useful cognitive skill that is needed for sketching, drafting and developing design ideas at a later age. This place-holding, seems to have potential as a pre-design skill as well as a pre-writing skill. There is a similar narrative process involved in an evolving design as there is in creating a storyline. If children can place-hold for storytelling at such a young age, then they should be able, later, to place-hold ideas for designing.

The place-holding of ideas through a mixture of graphics and text-symbols, which appeared as a staging-post towards literacy, has potential for recording of ideas in a range of contexts and applications. If children in their fifth year can use drawing and text so interactively to tell a story about playing in the garden at the weekend, for instance, then surely, this skill can be developed for generating and developing creative ideas across the primary school years, not just in art or design and technology lessons, but across the curriculum. This intuitive understanding of place-holding of developing ideas could function as a springboard for understanding how to use drawing to develop a design for making a product to fit a specific purpose, making quick sketches from different viewpoints, trying out different techniques or media, or using abstract relational graphs.

The following illustrative excerpt is from a video recording of four children (all aged around 5 years old) who were engaged in making pictures of a member of their family dressed up for a fancy dress party:

Kate:	Izzy, wizzy, let's get ... Mrs. H., I need one of ... pointy ... triangle.
Mrs. H.:	What will you use that for?
Kate:	Hat. Witch's hat.
Richard:	Her Mum's a witch!
Ellie:	If you used a square you could do some arms and legs on it, for like Iron Man.
Richard:	I'm going to draw him big. Bigger than those. *(Meaning the pre-cut shapes. Draws large square body on his page.)*
Mrs. H. to Joe:	What's that round shape going to be?
Joe:	It's for my brother in his football training. On his shirt ... er ... here ... it says ... like this *(waves hand as if drawing the team logo in the air)*. Last time, this boy, he had all red paint on him. It looked like blood. Where's the red? I'm going to do blood. Out his nose. All everywhere it went all down his socks.
Ellie:	Was it real blood or just paint?
Richard:	Iron Man has brown blood. It's called rust, you know.
Ellie:	Can I have blue, please? Thank you.
Kate:	W is M the other way up, isn't it Mrs. H.?
Richard:	I've got an alien bedroom.
Kate:	You haven't! Joe, have you got football bedroom?
Joe:	No. My brother's side has pictures.
Kate:	My witchy Mummy's going to have a broomstick. One way up she's Mummy and upside down, weeee, look, look, she's Witchie!
Richard:	Who wants brown? Who wants red? *(Standing up and sharing out the crayons.)* Here you are. You've got your crayons now! Don't drop them on the floor!
Ellie:	I'm wanting pink and yellow. Mrs. H. ...
Richard:	We can all share them all really.

It is clear from this short excerpt that the children are thinking interactively as they draw. They are each engaged in their own train of thought which runs parallel to the drawing activity, and even parallel to each other. Different verbalized ideas may trigger other ideas (Ellie's Iron Man idea is taken up by Richard) or completely ignored. This is clearly part of these children's daily interactions. Kate contradicts Richard's fantasy about his bedroom, which prompts Joe to make a very precise and truthful response to her question about his. He has picked up the clues from Ellie's querying of the paint/blood that the girls have strict ideas about what can be imaginary and what cannot. Richard's statement about Iron Man's blood, coupled with his enactment of giving out crayons, followed by the concession that they can all share, shows that he is comfortable switching between the world of his playful imagination and that of reality. Kate is playfully exploiting the mirror symmetry of the letters W and M for her 'witchy Mummy' who transforms from one to the other by flying upside down.

The children's conversation demonstrates how the activity of drawing develops within a social context. Although children also draw alone, especially at home, in school drawing is an activity that takes place in a social context in which the developing image is open to view and possible comment by other children and the teacher. Children frequently look at each other's drawings to copy or borrow images and stylistic details. For instance, outdoor scenes are indicated by a strip of blue sky along the top and a sun in the corner. This will develop into the presence of free floating clouds and V-shaped birds occupying the upper portion of the picture, or perhaps an aeroplane flying past. Indoor scenes often have a light hanging down to indicate that the top edge of the paper represents the ceiling. These context signals are an important short-hand in which to frame the picture and to be able to concentrate on developing the representation of the action or event being drawn. In order to be accepted and praised by peers as well as adults, children need to learn to produce and employ a set of graphic conventions. This enables reading of their picture by others and for conversations about the pictures to take place as they are being drawn.

Children are forced by circumstances to adopt and refine the accepted micro-cultural code for particular drawn forms. How do other children draw people? Is it better than their own? However, this peer pressure may mean that some children appear to revert to a more immature form of drawing in school in comparison to their output at home in order to 'fit in' with the expectations of the peer group in school. A gifted 5-year-old boy who had started to try to place one figure as if behind another figure produced only one such drawing at school (of parachutists descending, the strings crossing each other) but then noticed that everyone else drew their figures next to each other. In future, so did he. This, it seemed, was how children drew in school.

Drawing and telling stories

Although Piaget made a seminal contribution to the understanding of child development, where he was less successful was due to his view of the child as scientist, whereas the child was looking for the story underlying the puzzles and expecting that story to make sense. Piaget mistook the motivation and the mechanism, due to his own background as a scientist in an age and culture in which rationalistic science was considered to lead the perception of reality, rather than being just one of many ways of making sense of the world around us. The child's means of making sense of the world is frequently as narrative. Small children love stories and the more stories they are told, the better their ability to construct abstract concepts. Generally speaking, children from story-rich homes seem to do better in school. They know that meanings slide. They know that words can be used in several ways and can be interpreted at different levels. They know about metaphor and can extrapolate from the literal to the figurative. Their heuristic knowledge of the way we can use and interpret language enables story-rich children to access and utilize the symbol systems of the classroom, graphical and mathematical as well as linguistic.

The development of early creativity seems interwoven with the development of play and fantasy and the ability to manipulate inner mental images, not as simple discrete constructs, but as complex free-flowing, changing, kaleidoscoping, transforming and interconnecting with fuzzy boundaries which can collide, combine, spark off the new and the novel and create a whole new world of meaning and seeing, just like children's fantasy play. The mechanism that enables this richness is analogy and extrapolation: fitting new percepts into the inner story already created and stretching and extending those inner constructs to assimilate new ones where possible or to rearrange or even discard those constructs to accommodate new ideas which will not comfortably fit. Experience and knowledge provide the base ground for assessment of new percepts that are added to the knowledge base by finding an analogy to already stored concepts, which the brain stores as like/non-like. Language or visual symbols shortcut the process and enable storage and classification. Perception or recollection of the symbol may launch a whole raft of new concepts.

Some children become highly adept at telling stories through drawn rather than written form. Accompanying the creation of the drawing shown in Figure 2.3 (p. 62) represents an elaborate tale about a clown mouse that 6-year-old Jason made up and told to his friend Michael as he drew it. The written record of this story is contained in the title on

Figure 2.3   Jason's cat story

the left-hand page and the mouse's words 'Look a cat', yet the story-telling continued for more than half an hour. There should have been an audio recorder handy to capture this elaborate and imaginative tale. Jason could have listened again, redrafted and refined, all in drawing and speech, and eventually, if appropriate, the final telling could have been transcribed by an adult. The digital media revolution has put managing the hardware within the capability of quite young children, as well as the price being within the budget capacity of many schools.

A similar example, from an older child, is the illustration on the front cover of this book, which is an example of 8-year-old Randall's work. He was meant to be drawing a map of the Labyrinth to help Theseus escape from the Minotaur but found creating his own version of the tale through oral storytelling and drawing to be much more compelling.

For children like Jason and Randall, drawing can be used effectively as a means of drafting ideas that will be turned into text form later, thereby freeing the children from worrying about the mechanics of writing, accuracy of spelling and correct punctuation at the same time as trying to generate creative ideas. Drawings can be used to quickly record ideas holistically, rather than having to produce them in a chronological narrative sequence. Teaching the use of flow charts enables more complex stories to be built up and the child can then make decisions about the flow and outcomes. In this messy stage of story development, using a mix of drawn images, graphic symbols, connective lines and text, scrawled all over the paper, the child could produce a cohesive story frame quickly and then move on to worry about the spelling, grammar and punctuation afterwards. They would also be working more in the way that many adults plan written, graphic and mixed-media products, including full-length novels and information texts.

The large numbers of picture books available in Nursery, Reception and Key Stage 1 classes means that children are immersed in these genres from an early age, yet for some reason, this is not a genre that is greatly encouraged for children's own production. The pressure of end of key stage tests frequently means that children's own stories must be composed in correctly spelt words, full sentences and proper punctuation.

However, the range of early picture books represent a complex pattern of interaction between picture and text, which could provide rich models for children's own creative productions. For example:

- the picture may simply illustrate the text
- the text may comment on the picture
- picture and text may share the story, with some parts being developed in each
- the story may be told by the pictures with the text as commentary in a different voice
- the text may be juxtaposed and create tensions that demonstrate tensions within the story
- the text and graphics may be telling two versions of the same situation from two different perspectives (John Burningham's *Shirley* books)
- two sets of graphics: a large picture that complements the main plot text plus smaller pictures that provide a commentary, alternative perspectives or show what other characters are doing or thinking while the main plot is taking place. These are frequently slightly subversive, using humour or whimsy
- fully interactive graphic/text stories such as cartoons and manga.

Picture books demonstrate text and graphics in conversation. Unfortunately, it is often the case that in schools what is modelled and encouraged is a monologue. Teachers who have been taught only to think of story development as a text function do not model text/graphic interaction because this is not how they themselves think. It is important that children are taught to create and develop their thinking through graphic as well as written means, not only because of the intense power of graphic images, but also because increased globalization, coupled with exponentially increasing computer speed and data storage capacity, means that icons and graphics are becoming a primary means of communication. For instance, the accessibility of visual humour, its depiction of irony, and potential for social commentary, playing with facts and impressions, can actively develop children's critical thinking and reflective skills.

As children reach the end of their primary school years, they are becoming increasingly aware of the adult world, and want increasingly to discover the ways in which it functions. In school, children's understanding of the complexities of the adult world often come through studying history. Why did the Vikings come to Britain? Why did the French have a revolution and send their king and queen to the guillotine? These are questions about adult motives and actions that help children to develop a frame of reference against which to understand the contemporary adult social world (people migrate to improve their lifestyle; the desire for change spills over into anger and destructiveness). This understanding may exist at a sub-lingual, intuitive level that can be expressed through drawing. Combining this with an appropriate graphic form, whether the cartoon strip or a dual-graphic genre, children can construct a page of social commentary on the lives of the Egyptians, Tudors or Victorians. Humour, both visual and textual, can be used effectively to re-enforce concepts and understanding of how life was lived or of significant historical events. Such creative playfulness allows children time and space to absorb and reflect upon the ideas and information about the times that they are studying. Producing works of visual commentary develops children's ability to balance two things at once, to see and appreciate layers within the social world, and express two viewpoints at the same time. Even such a simple device as asking children to draw what each of the characters in a story might be thinking about at a certain point helps children to take on alternative perspectives and see the world through other eyes.

Drawing solutions

Realizing the analogical nature of drawing and the way in which lines can be used to mean many things, enables children to use drawing for the resolution of a whole range of visual and intellectual puzzles and representations. 'If the mind cannot solve a problem by terms dictated by the situation, then it will do so in terms of some other but similar situation. Thus invention is the emergence in the mind of novelty under the control of system' (Blanshard, 1964: 148).

Weldon (cited by Bruner, 1979) made a distinction between difficulties, puzzles and problems based on the way a problem is solved. The discovery of a solution for a problem consists of knowing how to impose a workable 'puzzle form' on its various difficulties, which converts the problem or difficulty into one with which we can deal. This applies in any context, whether using drawing to sort and classify scientific data through using a Venn diagram or trying to communicate the feeling of pleasurable observation. Since the links between concepts and problem situations are bi-directional, analogy and extrapolation from established skills and practised repertoires are an extremely useful problem-solving tool. By classifying problems according to the same umbrella concepts, problem situations can be translated into appropriate procedures. It would seem, therefore, that a central skill in problem-solving is to be able to link the appropriate strategy knowledge to the specific domain knowledge analogy with previously encountered problems.

For instance, knowing that a design problem can be solved through drawing is an imposition of a known puzzle form in Weldon's sense. Children are frequently unaware of the limits of their visualization skills. They think they have the answer and start to paint or make something, leave it half done because it does not work or change it completely at a whim. However, realizing that the task is bigger or more complex than can be visualized mentally and that external support is needed, whether by doing a drawing, making a list or other place-holding device, involves a level of self-awareness or meta-cognition which most Key Stage 1 children lack. By teaching children to objectify and record their mental images, to visualize onto paper, draw ideas before cutting into expensive materials, teachers are encouraging methodological efficiency for use in a whole range of contexts.

Key Stage 2 children can use drawing as a design or drafting medium because their greater mental agility and maturity enables them to perceive and exploit the analogy between the designing medium and the making medium. Although younger children can appreciate this connection, they cannot transfer seamlessly from one to the other, nor can they effectively manipulate one symbol system to develop ideas about something to be created in another. Arnheim (1969: 148) called these 'pictorial analogies' which 'fulfil a mediating position between the world of sensory experience and the disembodied forces underlying the objects and events of that experience'.

For the experts, with rich previous experience in solving like problems, the analogies are not far away. However, Barrett (1983) observed that novices often have difficulty employing analogies to solve problems due to difficulties identifying which of the problems they have already solved are conceptually similar to the one they are currently trying to solve. For novices, learners and children with limited experience of a range of drawing genres, the search may be too wide to provide useful links. They may well, therefore, be able to resolve problems relating to observational drawing but struggle to use drawing for more abstract meanings, such as those representing scientific relationships. Children frequently struggle to know which puzzle form they should apply, or which genre of drawing is appropriate. They will get the level of detail wrong or spend time putting in texture or shading detail when an outline sketch is all that is needed.

Decisions such as these about the puzzle form of the drawing are taken both *within* the process of drawing, as the image unfolds across the surface, and by thinking *with* or *through* the process of drawing itself as decisions are taken about the message that the drawing will convey. For instance, a child involved in drawing a cat asleep on a chair will be thinking about the layout of the drawing, how the different shapes and textures will be represented:

- How will the lines capture the relationship of the shapes of the cat against the back of the chair?
- How will the lines or shading convey furriness?
- Will the cushion look right or will it be at a funny angle so the cat looks as if it is about to slide off the chair?
- How will the lines on the page be read by others?
- Will they know what the lines are supposed to mean?

Depending on the age of the child, these questions will be answered differently. Upper Key Stage 2 children (ages 10–11 years) will try to use shading to convey the effect of light and shade that enable us to perceive the cat really sitting on the cushion. Younger children may distort the shapes as seen in order to convey their knowledge of cats, chairs and cushions. Making the cat's fur look fluffy is not just a satisfying thing to achieve, but is also about conveying to others what the perception means to the observer. This is not just any cat on any chair. This is a fluffy cat, sitting on a smooth round cushion on an upright chair. The meaning that is conveyed may be about the desire to touch, stroke and disturb the sleeping animal or it may be about enjoyment of observation of an animal totally at rest and unaware of the close watching, a secret, almost guilty, voyeurism.

It is frequently said that learning to draw is about learning to look and that through the process of drawing, knowledge, understanding and perception increase by the action of careful observation or construction from the imagination. Thus the formation of an idea, image or perception is enabled by the process of looking carefully and closely enough to be able to produce that image on paper. This is only partly true, even of observational drawing, as the hand needs to learn how to produce the image but, more importantly, there is a second thread to thinking *through* the process of drawing: the perception of meaning and decisions about its communication as the drawing develops. Drawing is not just a product or container for thought, it is also a process, a journey of thought development. It is the analogical and metaphorical nature of drawing that enables this process thinking to happen.

Summary

The exploration of this dimension of drawing ('Drawing to mean') has focused on the way in which drawing stands as a portal between the inner and outer reality, a bridge between the imagination and external perception of reality. This is true of all forms of drawing and, although examples have been taken from a range of drawing genres, the discussion has intentionally remained generic. The analogical, metaphorical and metonymic nature of drawing (both in process and as product) has been the continuing and linking thread throughout the discussion. Attaching intentional meaning to their drawing is one of the great leaps forward in the infant's developing consciousness, which continues to develop throughout the primary school years to the point at which the adolescent is sufficiently conscious of the metaphorical nature of the medium itself to choose purposely to exploit it.

As an analogue for thought, ideas, imagination, memory and perception, drawing acts as both an open door and as a gatekeeper. It is the imperative to make drawing 'mean' that acts as a brake on total anarchy and that pushes the infant from simply playing and exploring the sensuality of the materials and the enjoyment of the rhythmic process of mark-making to attributing symbolism to their output. Once a scribble is meant to be 'Mummy', then the race is on to make it look more like 'Mummy'. Once the drawing is meant to represent the warm furry cat asleep on the chair, the need is to convey the feeling, the observation, the knowledge of tactile sensations and three-dimensional form and substance, as well as the perceptions of angle and shadow from the viewer's perspective. All these perceptions have been filtered by the young artist's mind, and they cannot subtract their memories and knowledge from their current perceptions. What a drawing or the process of drawing means is inevitably influenced by the cultural semiotic system in which the child is being raised.

The metaphorical nature of drawing, as a way of *seeing as* in Wittgenstein's (1969) sense means that a drawing is frequently viewed and discussed as if it were the final product and then ideas about a mental image of a real object adapted in the light of the drawing of the mental image. Seeing the similarities and patterns in things enables the mental leap from one area of knowledge to another or from one symbol system to another. Further, in the context of designing, analogical fluency allows the construction of a pattern in one symbol system (the sketch or template) to aid the construction of the next stage of production in another (the macquette or mock-up). In this way the designer draws what is yet to be made and begins a journey whose end is off the page and continues through trial pieces and on into the completion of the final product.

Dimension 3

Drawing to feel

The third dimension of drawing to be explored in this book, 'Drawing to feel', encompasses the role of drawing in the development of children's affective, emotional responses to the world around them, whether this be to the external physical world, the social world or the inner personal world of their imagination. As stated in the 'Introduction: Drawing to think', each of the dimensions of drawing identified in this book overlap and intertwine, thus 'Drawing to feel' cannot be separated from other ways and forms of drawing. It would be a false assumption, therefore, for readers to think 'Oh, this is the art chapter, then' as if this were all that art is concerned about or that all drawings that express emotion must be art. The approach taken in discussing this dimension of drawing, therefore, is to outline the ways in which children use, and should be encouraged to use, drawing to develop their affective and emotional awareness and capacities.

This is not separate from meaning; the two are intertwined, as are all the dimensions of drawing. For instance, Michael Holt (1971: 7) posed the question 'What is the interplay between painting and sculpture on the one hand and mathematics on the other?', and provided his answer in the statement 'The one is something we appreciate with our eyes and respond to with our emotions and the other with our minds and our intellect'. However, the distinction is not that clear cut, as his book *Mathematics and Art* itself demonstrates. Raney (1998: 39) speaks of the empowerment, passion and delight that is part of our interaction with the visual world, for which 'the driving force is prior expectation of meaning'. This dimension, 'Drawing to feel', explores the way in which the process of drawing enables the exploration and development of affective meaning and perception.

Historically speaking, however, the overwhelmingly greater part of research into children's drawings has been into drawing as a finished likeness of an observation, rather than into drawing as a process or as an emotional response to a situation or observation. 'Progress' in

children's artistic achievement has, likewise, often been seen as acquisition of the skills that enable the representation of the photo-realism
of single point perspective, without a clear notion that single point perspective is just one artistic genre among many that happened to be
given high status within a particular culture at a particular time in
Europe (and then America) from about the mid-fourteenth century
onwards until the rise of 'modern' art in the early twentieth century.
Not only is this a naive view of art, extremely limited in respect to
artistic output worldwide, but it also ignores artistic process and intent,
whose primary aim is often to stimulate a deep affective and spiritual
response in the viewer.

The desire to break away from the shackles of the established genres
and to say something more through art was the prime mover in such
movements as the development of British landscape painting at the
turn of the nineteen century (for example, Constable and Turner),
Impressionism in France, and the reassessment of the Western artistic
heritage that led to the development of abstract and conceptual art in
the twentieth century. When looking at art with children, it is important to encourage them to consider how the work makes them *feel* in
order to capture its inner affective and aesthetic qualities. Drawing or
painting in the style of Van Gogh, in paint or pastel, for instance,
should include a careful examination and discussion of his use of brush
strokes in different directions to create the feeling of seeing the dark
trees against the sky. His drawing of his chair and his room can be con-
trasted with photographs of chairs and bedrooms to discuss the way in
which he distorts perspective in order to say more about the room and
his chair than if he had simply drawn a single point perspective view.
Such discussion also helps children to understand that the aim of many
artists was not to produce photographic likeness, but to say something
more important about their own feelings and responses (in this case,
Van Gogh's happiness in his new home) through their choice of colour,
brushwork and manipulation of multiple viewpoints.

People look in art for something in the work that touches them, that
elicits an emotional response, a meeting between artist and viewer. It
was this that delighted Klee and Mondrian in the art of young children
and caused them to compile great collections of children's drawings.
What they were seeking was to capture the purity of the uneducated,
pure response; affective, not intellectualized.

Koestler (1974) distinguished between participatory emotions, which
are passive and yet cathartic (weeping, laughing, and so on) and com-
batorial ones, which agitate or exclude (such as anger or spite). He says:
'The participatory emotions ... [involve] an expansion of consciousness

by identification processes of various kinds' (Koestler, 1974: 286). Even when negative emotions are expressed, for instance in Picasso's *Guernica*, works of art aim to draw in the viewer to a particular sympathy with the subject, to develop an understanding of circumstances, narrative or concept. Art has a social function, to communicate at an affective as well as an intellectual level, such that viewers become participants in the artist's eye view with their cognitive and emotional perspective.

A large part of artistic output worldwide and across time has been religious and aims to communicate spiritual values and aspirations or to inspire contemplation. Our earliest surviving evidence of art on a large scale, such as that preserved through the special conditions of caves in Spain or the desert in South Africa, show art that was probably used for religious purposes. The huge animals on the cave walls, perhaps, represent what people believed they saw as they explored the depths of the cave with rush lamps in hand or in shamanic trances while in the caves. Perhaps, the shapes appeared in the flickering gloom, leading people to believe the caves were inhabited by the departed spirits of the animals on whose fecundity their lives depended. Later, perhaps even centuries later, the shapes were outlined and painted as the cave became an important religious site for a people with power and wealth to employ artists to delineate them. We cannot know, only muse and speculate. Even until the last 200 years in European cultures, the human ability to be creative was seen as being divinely inspired, and the verb 'to create' implied creation from nothing.

Howe et al. (2001) ascribed a spiritual sense to both the appreciation of designed artefacts and to the act of designing itself. They draw attention to the sense of wonder experienced within such man-made structures as cathedrals or temples, or even in response to well-crafted smaller artefacts, such as watches, inlaid furniture and so on. The 'wow factor' that is experienced when viewing such products can also be applied to drawings (Leonardo da Vinci's detailed sketches of the human body, for instance). More radically, Howe et al. suggest that children's own work can evoke a spiritual sense in others. Feeling and expressing appreciation of each other's work creates an affirmative experience that enhances each child's sense of self-worth within their community. This, claim Howe et al. is not just a social experience, but also a spiritual one.

The sensuality of mark-making

There is something deeply sensual about the act of mark-making, in both the physical relishing of the materials and in the act of making marks with them. There is the sensuous feel of wax crayons, the crispness of new paper, the smell of paints. There is even something magical about a new rubber, especially if it has a television hero printed on it. Little girls become excited by glitter pens and rainbow pencils. There is the delight (or abhorrence) in getting messy; in the gloopy feel of finger paints or the cold dampness of clay. There is the smell and feel of the packaging, of a new box of crayons, the excitement and stimulation of a new sketchbook, the myriad colours and textures that seem to promise new vistas of creative opportunity.

Within much of Van Gogh's work, for instance, can be seen the sensual experience of colour and form and of the movement of the brush on the canvas. His spiralling clouds, curvaceous cypresses, bold brush strokes and bright colours depicting his room with the chair and bed speak of a visionary longing for a world of joy, in contrast to the real world with its round of frustrations and disappointments. Hundertwasser's riotous colours, like technicolour doodles, also display a revelling in the process of laying down line and colour. Seurat, despite proclaiming the scientific basis for his technique, conveys a fundamental delight in his miriad dots of pure colour. There is a satisfaction in the balance in Mondrian's abstract works or a jarring in some of Picasso's portraiture that the viewer responds to at a subliminal level that is to do with a feeling of pleasure, almost despite themselves at times, for what the artist is trying to understand and convey by the arrangement of both positive and negative shapes, size and proportion, colour combinations and contrasts, tone and shading (or lack of it). Adult artists choose and use visual clues, codes and signs to convey the underlying message of their work in ways that children are unable to do. However, the jaunty or drooping line, the choice of colours, patterning or arrangements of elements of the work can be used effectively, albeit intuitively, by children. It was this that artists such as Klee sought within their work.

As well as the sensual delight in the physical properties of the materials, there is also the enjoyment of the physical sensation of drawing, of moving the drawing instrument across the paper and making marks. This is a combination of the satisfaction of mastery, of control and the ability to use the medium as a form of expression, of coming to understand, represent, clarify, resolve, maintain or express ambiguity. Thus when the infant is scribbling round and round on the paper, making brrmm-brmm noises as they do so, they are enjoying the way the materials handle and feel, refining through experience the amount of pressure needed to make a mark with the tool, while also feeling the emotional enjoyment and satisfaction in mark-making, both in terms of the bodily sensation and the proto-representational resolution of intent. The enjoyment of drawing, of the process of creating marks on paper, motivates the youngest children to experiment. The sense of mastery of tools, techniques and materials provides its own pleasure. This enjoyment may be conveyed in the use of colour, by means of the arrangement of the elements of the picture or by the inclusion of well-practised repertoires, such as the yellow sun in a top corner.

Older children find this simple satisfaction with the process of drawing much harder to capture. By age 7, some children have already become too self-critical of the products of their drawing activities to enjoy the process for its own sake. At age 5 or 6 years, children will complete a picture with a smile or sigh of satisfaction. They have completed what they set out to do at the time and there is a sense of positive closure to the activity. Unfortunately, for many children, as they move through Key Stage 2, the dissatisfaction with the *product* begins, to rob them of their enjoyment of the *process*. This can be a difficult time. Parents and teachers know that further practice is necessary to improve technique and develop skills, but also children's own increased clarity of observational skills and imagination that created the mental image that they wanted the picture to look like seems increasingly at odds with what they are able to produce with their hands. Sensitive discussion of the nature of the product as well as good quality teaching of process is vital at this stage. The feeling of dissatisfaction and disappointment with their results is normal at this age and discussion of the feeling and its causes is more productive than simply telling children their work is 'good' when their own inner instincts tell them it falls short of their desire and intention.

Children frequently think that works of art, like literature and music, were written at a single attempt. They do not understand the need for drafting, revision and redrafting that the artist, writer or composer imposes upon themselves in order to create such works. Monet destroyed many of his attempts at capturing the water lilies floating on his pond because he did not want what he viewed as substandard work being sold. Van Gogh's mental instability was caused through the tension he felt between his inner vision and the struggle to capture it on canvas. Dissatisfaction is, unfortunately, an essential ingredient of high-level creativity. It may help children to know that this self-criticism is part of growing up and is an essential part of learning to be an artist, writer or musician. Without becoming self-critical, progress comes to a halt. The feelings of disappointment along the way can either become a spur to further application to the field or the trigger to abandoning the attempt.

The role of adults and peers in offering constructive and practical support is vital. Children have a limited repertoire. Showing them ways that artists have resolved visual representational problems through developing a particular style or employing a particular genre can be of help. Picasso reinvented himself constantly over the course of his long career. Understanding the way in which artists employed different forms of expression to match the specific problems they were trying to resolve at the time can enable children to understand that there are no right or wrong ways to draw or paint. Developing a series of lessons on the theme of, say, Cubism, allowing children to experiment with the genre in both two and three dimensions, allows the development of penmanship, visual literacy and an alternative way of looking at the world, without the problems that attempting complete visual realism can present.

Creativity as affective flow

The origins of creativity may be traced to the infant's first explorations of the world around them. Bailey (1971: 118) asserted that 'the basis of creativity is need, a need to know and express feeling, a need to come to terms with what is already known and what is only partly known'. This is closely tied to the child's need to explore, which underpins their scientific search, seen first in an infant's grasping at objects, and the feelings of pleasure in exchanges with significant adults.

Csikszentmihalyi (2002) depicted the state of intense engagement as a state of 'flow' in which the awareness of the passing of time seems to diminish as the level of involvement deepens. He observed this state of flow when people were absorbed in creative activity. In a state of flow, the creative person becomes unaware of external circumstances, noise and the doings of other people. Concentration intensifies and they lose their self-consciousness as they become completely absorbed in the process of creation:

> Concentration is so intense that there is no attention left over to think about anything irrelevant, or to worry about problems. Self-consciousness disappears, and the sense of time becomes distorted. An activity that produces such experiences is so gratifying that people are willing to do it for its own sake, with little concern about what they will get out of it, even when it is difficult or dangerous. (Csikszentmihalyi, 2002: 71)

In this state of flow, a person becomes cocooned in a self-absorbed state from which the creative act proceeds. This is not an adults-only phenomenon, as can be readily observed in children at play, as they consciously suspend their sense of reality and become totally absorbed in the play, in its rules, roles and resolution. This is directly parallel to the artist or designer's experience. Indeed, the same cognitive and affective processes are operating. The emotional satisfaction that emanates from such total involvement in the process triggers the flow of endomorphines that not only give pleasurable positive feedback, but may produce physical effects such as a slowing of the heartbeat and lowering of stress levels.

Csikszentmihalyi reported that in the studies in which he was involved, all flow activities had in common:

> a sense of discovery ... transporting the person into a new reality. It pushed the person into higher levels of performance, and led to previously undreamed-of states of consciousness. In short, it transformed the self by making it more complex. In this growth of the self lies the key to flow activities. (2002: 74)

Thus creativity has been linked to well-being, physical, mental and emotional. This is not to say that these episodes of flow necessarily feel pleasurable at the time. Someone may be grappling with contradictions and problems that are draining of both physical energy and inner strength. At the extreme ends of the spectrum, in cases of outstanding genius, the ability to cope with the intensity of the process has sometimes caused mental breakdown. However, for the vast majority of the population and for children in school, the deep involvement in the creative process is a source of feelings of well-being and personal satisfaction. This sense of empowerment, of being able to create something oneself, in whatever medium or situation, is emotionally healthy.

For adults as well as children, drawing can perform such a function in a unique way, since it does not require language. The parts of the brain that are active while people are drawing appear to be primarily the emotional, sub-linguistic areas. Damasio (2003) suggests that emotional circuits of the brain are engaged before the intellectual. The parts that switch on first and relate directly to sensory perception precede comprehension. The act of responding with the hand to the act of seeing may link directly with these emotional centres of brain activity, which in turn triggers the release of chemicals within the brain that are related to emotional states rather than to the stimulation of language-based reasoning. These more primitive acts of brain functioning are closer to the experiences of other creatures and satisfy more primeval needs than those activities that are language based. Even mathematicians and logicians, who appear to be concerned with the most cerebral of human activity, seek and feel an inner satisfaction and deep pleasure in the sense of beauty that they find in a particular formula or proof of a theorem.

When drawing, the intense focusing of concentration, whether of looking at an external scene in order to reproduce it as accurately as possible on paper, or the externalization of inner images and memories, tends to shut out distracting thoughts and worries about other things. This is especially true of the young child or the experienced adult, neither of whom have inhibitions about the quality of their product in relation to the output of others. The experience of drawing is less comfortable, however, for those who feel constantly that their output is less worthy than others around them. Putting up children's work on the wall for all to see should only happen in consultation with the child. What may appear cute and child-like to an adult could be a source of extreme embarrassment to the child. Unfortunately, the biggest inhibitor to a child's affective flow might just be to publicly endorse it.

Patterning

Islamic religious architecture has explored and exploited the use of patterning to express sublime beauty in a unique way. Within the rows of tiles that line the walls of the mosques of Pakistan or Turkey are riots of repeated symmetrical designs. The intoxicating assault on the senses that is the experience of entering the world of Islamic tiled spaces is deeply satisfying at an emotional and spiritual level. It hits home to part of the human psyche through the perception and resolution of complex patterning. No other culture has developed such sophisticated use of line, colour and tessellation that combines mathematical simplicity with figural complexity. However, this sense of visual delight in complex mathematical patterns within these mosques also has a spiritual dimension. The aim of the designers was to celebrate and express the beauty of worship and of Allah himself. This interaction of spatial precision and linear complexity speaks to the spiritual and emotional capacities before also speaking to the intellectual and rational. The tessellating patterns of the shapes, as well as the decoration and adornment of individual tiles, play games with sight and reason, using crosses and stars or octagons and squares to augment the complex symmetry of the overlaying surface patterns. When studying Islamic practices, children should be given the opportunity to look at the tile patterns and to attempt to draw some of them.

The act of drawing enables the children to appreciate the complexity of the patterns and the way in which the symmetries interact to create the tessellating patterns. The tiles themselves are often made in complex tessellating shapes and it may help to provide the children with templates that fit neatly onto 1 cm squared paper, at a scale of, say, one tile fitting across six squares. The children can then position the tiles accurately and explore the possibilities of the kind of symmetrical designs used on the tiles. This kind of close observational and experimental drawing develops children's appreciation of the complexities of the tile patterns while also developing their own understanding of the interaction between symmetry and tessellation.

A less complex starting point for younger children might be American quilt patterns. Whichever is chosen, it is important that children draw and create, not just look. Appreciation of the way in which the patterns are created and built up can only come through the careful study and personal involvement required through drawing them rather than passively looking.

The desire to see pattern in the world around us is intuitive and primeval. Most viewers of work by Jackson Pollock seek to make sense of the maze of overlaid lines and scribbles through looking for patterns. The desire to make meaning and see patterns runs deep, and is satisfying once found. An infant's first attempts at controlled movements of a pen often have within them a sense of pattern and regularity as the child grips a pen in full fist and makes backwards and forwards motions followed by round and round ones, even if these are not initially intentional pattern-making but the inevitable result of the arm movement. The infant's intention is to gain control of the pen in three quite specific ways: up and down, side to side and round in circles.

Children's ability to perceive and consciously construct patterns appears to develop with their ability to count. At around age 5 years, as they develop the ability to see numbers as abstract entities, they become able to string beads in simple 1–1 colour or shape patterns. Children whose mathematical and linguistic capabilities are less well developed will continue to string the beads randomly, even if an adult begins the string for them with alternating colours. By the end of Year 1 (age 6) many children have begun to gain specific pattern vocabulary (dotty, stripy, zigzag and so on) thus demonstrating the ability to classify regular abstract formations. They also begin, at this age, to apply patterns within their own drawings. This may be applied decoration (for example, Hayley's butterfly, Figure 3.1) or as whole-page designs, although this is rarer. Young children want their drawing to be 'of' something. Playing with abstraction develops as true doodling develops, in young adolescence.

This developing perception of pattern in the social and physical worlds begins to show itself in children's drawings and is usually well developed by age 7. Trees may be uniformly long thin brown rectangles with round green tops. When branches are represented, they may be evenly arranged, springing from the top of the brown rectangle with the leaves positioned neatly along the length of the branch. Figure 3.2 is an example by a Year 5 girl (age 10 years) of the enjoyment of patterning

Figure 3.1   Hayley's butterfly

Figure 3.2   Trees by Year 5 girl

overriding a desire for realism, drawn as a result of making observations from a rooftop play area.

Girls, especially, are interested in fashion details on clothing and this is often the way that they begin to demonstrate the distinction between people in pictures. Stripes, wavy lines and spots appear on both male and female figures drawn by boys as well as girls between ages 5 and 7, and the more linguistically precocious may start to do this younger than their peers. However, this should not be taken as a guide of intellectual capacity or artistic capability. Once a technique appears within a group or class of children, the others quickly copy and the new technique is tried out and explored by all. The initial stimulus could come through social contact, observing an older sibling or other relative, a babysitter or even a casual meeting between children of different ages at a party, holiday club or airport lounge could be responsible for the new move forward.

The child has realized their capacity for using drawing to represent specific but infinitely variable instances as well as generalizations. The figures may look just the same as before in form but the essential addition of a patterned skirt or striped shirt has changed the figure from *a person* to *this person*. This is a major step towards the locational realism discussed in 'Dimension 4: Drawing to see'. Patterning, therefore, may be seen as one of the markers towards the ability to record specific observations, which, together with different side views of people, location in landscape and a more realistic use of colour, indicate that symbolism is being sacrificed to realism.

A less obvious form of patterning is the arrangement of the objects on the paper. Younger children, especially, draw what to them is the most important feature of the drawing first at a visually satisfying position on the page. If the drawing is to be of one object, it will be placed centrally on the paper. If children are drawing a scene containing several objects, a person outside their house for instance, then the objects that they have in mind at the start of the drawing will be arranged in a visually satisfying pattern with respect to each other. The position and size of subsequent objects are decided with respect to the positions of existing objects on the page. Since the child considers the whole process as unique and completed in one attempt, this positioning is vitally important to get right. Children's dissatisfaction with their drawings may stem, not just from the form of the objects that they draw, but from their positioning on the page, especially in relation to the size of other objects. They are beginning to grapple with pattern versus observation. They are aware that nearer objects appear larger than further ones but do not know how to represent this on paper. The neat pattern of 'sky above, earth below' is in conflict with their observation of trees in middle distance being 'higher' and 'smaller' than houses close to.

One way of helping children in upper Key Stage 2 (ages 10–11) may be through introducing drafting and redrafting. The objects in the first drawing could be cut out and arranged on a fresh sheet of paper to the child's satisfaction. Younger children will be happy just to glue the cut-out drawings onto a collage background, but older and more capable children in Key Stage 2 can be encouraged to redraw their picture in response to their observations and feelings about their draft. Getting the arrangement of the objects right to their personal satisfaction empowers the children to exploit their sense of visual patterning while also allowing for their developing sense of the need for realism.

Revealing inner states

Asking people to draw has become one of the tools used by psychoanalysts for disclosing patients' states of minds and emotional preoccupations. This is less effective for the sophisticated adult than for the innocent child, who is unaware of the adult's game and of the potential of drawings to reveal their inner feelings and cannot, as an adult might, consciously play a game with the analyst and disguise their true thoughts and feelings. However, only those especially trained and experienced in such psycho-analytical techniques should attempt to read too much into the content of children's drawings, especially if, for instance, specifically seeking evidence of a less than happy home situation, and under no circumstances should implications be drawn from a single drawing.

Occasionally, a child will produce a drawing that is remarkably telling of the observations that a teacher has made of a child over a period of time and a particular drawing may illustrate just the assessment that the teacher has made of a child. If a teacher is seriously concerned about the content of a child's pictures over an extended period of time, then, after consultation with senior management, discussion with social service colleagues may be appropriate. On no account should steps be taken by a teacher to confront or intervene in a child's home life on the basis of the content of children's drawings. Using drawing to clarify their developing knowledge of the appearance and function of the private parts of the human body is normal. Children have unbridled imaginations and delight in larger than life figures and representations. Their appetite for the gory and brutal often shocks adults, but is tempered by their lack of understanding that such things might be literally true. Children who have had real experiences of cruelty tend to produce very stilted rather than visually exciting drawings.

For instance, one child, who came from a family with a history of mental disturbance that included instances of extreme violence, very rarely produced figurative drawings at age 5 years. He used pencils to produce patches of colour, randomly placed on a sheet of paper, yet became totally absorbed in this action and refused to stop the activity before he was ready to do so. When he did produce images, these were contorted line drawings of isolated 'tadpole' figures. He was fascinated by violent computer games, and constantly role-played being one of these violent 'heroes'. How much of the imagery that he drew reflected the real circumstances at home or how far it was a reflection of his fascination with violent fantasies was impossible for his teacher to tell. The violence of his outrage at having to stop his activity for playtime or lunchtime, was as worrying and suggestive of the turmoil of his inner emotional and psychological state as his output on paper.

It is inadvisable, however, to take just a child's drawings as external evidence, as two people may make completely different interpretations of them, based on differing views of the child. A further anecdote will serve as illustration.

Sam's home life was not happy. It was rumoured among the learning support assistants (mostly local women) that his mother had a drink problem. He was not very clean and had a constantly runny nose, which did not win friends or endear him to his teachers. When his class began Year 2 (age 6+), their new teacher asked them to draw self-portraits to decorate the classroom. She was already finding Sam difficult to get to know. Exasperated, she strode into the staffroom, waving his sheet of paper. 'This is all he's done in an hour!' she announced loudly to the room. On the sheet was the outline of a face and two lines for a neck. Nothing more. No eyes, nose, or mouth. She had read the drawing as a sign of Sam's naughtiness, time-wasting and laziness. A colleague read it as a sign of his self-image being so poor that he saw himself as a blank. But perhaps he was just so conscious of his inability to deal with his runny nose and mucky face, that had attracted so much negative attention from his previous teacher, that he feared his face would be equally unacceptable to the new teacher and so did not dare risk presenting her with a picture of it. Perhaps he reasoned that being told off for laziness was the better option, with less potential for hurt from an adult into whose charge he was being entrusted for the foreseeable future. Whose reading of Sam's failure to draw in his features was right was, of course, impossible to know. It was, however, apparent to all, without reading anything into his drawing, that Sam was not, at that stage in his life, a happy little boy.

The underlying assumption of childhood innocence coupled with the belief that children find drawing fun and enjoyable leads to the conclusion that children's exploration of negative emotions and situations is an aberration and cause for concern. These assumptions do not necessarily hold and a child may use drawing to model and explore an emotional range that is at the edge of, or even beyond, their normal day-to-day experience. Children faced with anger, sadness, spite or cruelty, within themselves as well as within others, may use drawing as a means to enable them to resolve these tensions and contradictions. Such drawings may be of cartoon characters involved in acts of violence or may appear to glamorize negative feelings and actions. In the aftermath of the destruction of the World Trade Centre, children all around the globe drew twin towers with aeroplanes crashing into them, even those too young to understand what had happened. They knew from the way it was repeatedly shown on television and the reactions of the adults around them that this was a highly charged event. By drawing it or building it with plastic bricks and re-enacting the moment of impact, they were attempting to make sense and come to terms with something that deeply bothered them and which they were at a loss to understand.

Drawing may also be used by children as a means of escape from negative influences and surroundings. The art of Jewish children during World War II (Milton, 1989) is surprisingly free of representations of the deprivations that they were suffering. Many pictures are of religious or optimistic subjects such as gardens and outings, as if the children were using the opportunity to confirm their shared identity and invoke memories and hope of happier days.

Developing empathy

Although children may not be able to describe their emotions in words, this does not, of course, mean that they do not feel strongly about a whole range of issues. This basic human ability to respond to how others feel can be seen in young children's tendency to cry because others are crying or laugh with everyone, regardless of whether they understand the joke. The child's developing empathy with others grows with their widening experience of the world. By mid-childhood (ages 9–11) children are beginning to hold and express strong feelings about a range of issues that have touched their sympathy and anger. Fears and tears about big issues, such as child poverty or climate change and whether there 'will be a world by the time I'm forty', are well articulated by age 10, by which time, their growing awareness of the wider world includes the plight of children in other places (refugees, famine victims) and other times (for example, Victorian children down the mines).

Children's empathy for others can frequently be developed more powerfully through drawing than through writing. The mechanics of writing are too challenging for an early writer to be able to express complex emotions at the same time. Their greater fluency in drawing allows a child to reflect on the experience of the people they are depicting. The desire for realism and pictorial accuracy that blossoms from age 7 onwards means that the child must increasingly engage with the reality of the lives of the people and animals or with the features of the landscape or environment that they are drawing. As the picture takes form, so the child is able to reflect more and more deeply on the issues that are being portrayed, and their emotions become increasingly engaged with the scenario. The initial hazy impression has given way to a clearer and sharper image as the child begins a dialogue with the drawing, thinking about the landscape or townscape, considering how to render unfamiliar clothing or vehicles, and how to convey what the people look like.

By the end of Key Stage 2, children can begin to think about how to best convey the feelings of the people. Younger children may be able to convey happiness or sadness, but their graphic range is not sufficiently developed to be able to convey frustration, fear or despair. Occasionally, almost by accident, younger children will be able to convey shades of emotion by the stance of a figure or the angle of the arms, but this is more by serendipity than by conscious graphic design. Although able to recognize and appreciate these emotions, children may be uncertain about how people would react in a given situation as well as being unable to convey these emotions in graphic means.

Before the rise of the desire for visual realism, a young child will probably produce their current schema for the human figure in every situation, with little variation and with apparent disregard for the emotional impact of the scenario in which they are situated. This does not mean that the child is unaware of the way that the people would be feeling, nor does it mean that even quite young children should not be encouraged to use drawing to record scenes from the past or from other countries or cultures. The sheer act of drawing encourages reflectiveness, as the child becomes immersed in imagining the scene that they are recording. The act of drawing re-enforces to the child their thoughts and feelings as they draw and the completed drawing acts as a reminder of their emotional response.

Drawing has the potential to affirm previously held feelings and beliefs, to enable exploration of new feelings and to develop empathy and understanding. However, there may be dissonance and conflict between previously held beliefs (perhaps gleaned from friends or derived from family values) and the viewpoint expressed and endorsed by teachers and other education workers. This is particularly likely to occur over emotive issues connected to the most basic difference of human experience: race, religion, migration, causes of poverty and so on. The act of drawing may provide a means by which children may become conscious of the differences in viewpoint between home and school, and therefore experience a conflict of loyalties, which the act of drawing may highlight more than resolve.

Expressing humour

Children's humour is different to that of adults and so humour of a kind that an adult might appreciate is unlikely to be found in children's drawings. This does not mean that children do not use drawing to record things that they find funny or to develop and communicate an amusing storyline. A picture that appears to have no humorous content, to an adult's perception might, on consultation with the child, turn out to be a source of great merriment. Children's humour can be very dark and exploit fantasies of wickedness and sexuality. Within drawing, such dark themes are frequently hidden from accidental viewing by adults through use of multi-purpose stereotypical and symbolic imagery. A boy and girl standing together outside a house, for instance, may be suggestive of sexual liaison. Humour may also be found in the rude bits, the drawing of breasts and genitalia, which are the subject of adult censorship and stern disapproval. Children find furtive fun in creating these images as they dally with their awareness of sexuality and eroticism and its censorship within their society.

Visual humour depends on departure from the norm, on incongruence or on a surprise. It also requires the development of a repertoire of skills and conventions for expressing emotion through drawing, which essentially constitutes the learning of a culturally agreed symbolic language. Therefore, before the age at which children produce drawings that accurately represent observed realism, visual humour will appear to be missing from their output. There are few visual surprises in the stereotypical images of young children's drawings, where one well-practised image serves a multitude of visual texts. A secure knowledge of how the world works and the degree of flexibility of the rules by which the social world runs is required before these rules can be played with and a challenge recorded.

By age 6, children regularly draw pictures of situations or occurrences that they find funny. Children's sense of humour at this age centres on physical mishaps rather than linguistic contradictions and misjuxtapositions. A child may draw a picture of a man and a car, with something in his hand that has lots of lines coming from it, and explain the picture to an adult as 'This is my Dad when he went to wash the car and the water went all down him' and collapse into giggles. However, without the recounting of the tale, the picture is difficult to identify as funny. At this age, children have a fairly limited repertoire of images and patterns that they can employ with confidence and their ability to manipulate these precisely with humorous intent is equally limited, so that their pictures do not contain visual jokes that are immediately recognizable by an adult without an explanation of context.

Children's understanding and appreciation of visual humour, especially slapstick, is well developed by age 7, whereas their ability to manipulate formal language in order to create linguistic incongruence is nascent.

Although even infants can appreciate and exploit the limitations of other people's knowledge of a particular situation in order to create humour, before the age of 10 many children rely on shared knowledge of the incident rather than seeing a need to have all the information being woven into the text of the picture itself in a way that is readable by others beyond this circle of knowledge. However, children are usually drawing for an audience that can be assumed to know the incident in question. It is in conversation with teachers and others less close to the incident that children begin to realize the level of detail and specificity required to tell the tale to those not present.

Funny pictures are often produced in social situations, for example by a group of children drawing and talking together in relaxed circumstances. A comment by one child will spark off another and a humorous narrative will develop, with elements of it appearing in different children's drawings. Asking one of the children what their drawing is about will elicit laughter within the group and the individual will tell a little of the story, often with much giggling and appeal to others for support and corroboration. The narrative has developed as a shared story that sometimes crosses the boundaries of the risqué and was not intended for adult ears. Asking one child what their drawing is about is problematic. The drawing represents part of a spontaneous, jointly constructed storyline that has taken on a life of its own and each individual is barely able to remember which part they were drawing on their paper and which part is on a friend's paper. The whole series of drawing, produced by all the children, contains the story, constructed in conversation, with the drawing used as a support for the construction and illustration of the ongoing development of the narrative.

By age 10 some children will have sufficient manual dexterity and eye for detail to begin to express humour with their own drawings, which do not depend on the establishment of shared meanings for understanding. However, it is between the ages of 10 and 12 that children really begin to experiment with visual jokes. Matthews (2002) provides a delightful example by his son, showing a robot mounting a ladder to fight. Already on the platform is another robot being dispatched by a hero, and the climbing robot has an expression of resigned acceptance of his inescapable fate, tinged with the regret that to be a robot is to be programmed to the task. Matthews rightly comments on the remarkable characterization in this drawing. It demonstrates his son's awareness of the psychology of humour and of the role of the incongruent. His metacognition, of conscious understanding of how thinking works, as well as his manual dexterity and capability with a pencil, has developed sufficiently to be able to construct an image that comments on the incongruity of a self-aware robot. Few children will produce an image of such sophistication at such a young age.

Social rules and conventions are frequently the focus of visual humour through cartoons, both animated and in print. Infants may find animated cartoons frightening rather than funny, and be disconcerted by adults and older children laughing at cats being sliced up and joined back together again, for example. They have realized that such actions in the real world would kill the cat and cannot see anything funny about it. They are reading the drawings as if they represent the characters and objects in a more real way than the cartoon genre dictates. The young child does not yet know the genre's conventions in terms of the interaction of reality and fantasy. Once they realize that this is all a fantasy world, then they too can share in the joke and children may choose cartoon characters as their first vehicle to explore the portrayal of humour. As well as this being the most common genre in which they themselves will have seen visual humour, it would seem that the stylized rendering of well-known characters allows a structured framework in which to develop one area of visual thinking.

However, children rarely depart from or reverse the scripts already provided for the characters, so that, for instance, it would be unusual for a Key Stage 1 child to draw a character, known for its temerity, sitting down for lunch while a threatening character cowers under the table. Correct knowledge of the characters and storylines are important social currency and immersion into the cultural dialogue is a necessary prerequisite. Adults, even those interested in child art, frequently do not appreciate the socio-cultural role of cartoons, television programmes and themed toys in developing a shared cultural script for children's play. Strangers in airport lounges become immediate friends over an action figure, a hand-held games machine or even a set of television-themed felt pens and notepad. Being able to draw these characters realistically earns the admiration of peers; overtly subverting the genre by dallying with alternative visual readings and representations could be social suicide.

This shared cultural knowledge enables children to create pictures with shared cultural references of which adults are often barely aware. Early writers on child art often derided cartoons and the drawing of such images as derivative and 'copying' and, therefore, something that should be firmly discouraged in school. The purposeful devaluing of children's cultural heritage in this way is likely to be counterproductive and alienating of many of the children whom the school finds hardest to reach. The intellectual snobbery that dismissed cartoons as a debased form of art was inadvertently dismissing a powerful means of using drawing to express humour and social comment. The simplicity of a line drawing enables the comment or joke to be made and communicated effectively. Visual jokes are rare in oil painting and 'high art', and are all but missing in European sculpture after the gargoyles of the Middle Ages. 'High art' was not intended to be fun. It frequently served a serious political purpose, promoting the interests of just the people that caricaturists such as Hogarth targeted. It is this history of subversion through humour that leads the cartoon into condemnation as well as its position as spanning the edges of both literature and art. In recent years, Japanese manga and sophisticated animation techniques have pushed graphic storytelling into the mainstream.

Art, music and poetry

The emotional registers of art, music and poetry overlap and can be combined in a variety of ways, from reflective individual responses to tonal music to the vibrancy of musical theatre. The richness of combining the written word with illustration or pattern can be seen in such diverse places as in the tombs of the Pharaohs or in the rich traditions of medieval European illuminated manuscripts. The complexity of Celtic linear design, for instance, in the book of Kells or Lindisfarne Gospels, is part of the rich cultural heritage of the British Isles. Any study of the history of Britain between AD 500–1500 should include the examination of these remarkable documents that reveal the artistic abilities of people of past ages living in this country, most of whose names are totally unknown to us. The designs are frequently of deep mathematical complexity but providing children with squared paper, rulers and compasses should enable them to copy some of them and create their own. However, study of illuminated manuscripts should not just focus on the technical competence needed to create them but also on the spiritual and emotional impact of the designs, including the choice of colours.

Drawing and writing can be combined through illustrated calligraphy. Once children can produce a good hand in a standardized style, they can experiment with different fonts. Their knowledge of word-processing can help here and they can print out a complete alphabet in a range of fonts to try out before choosing one to go with a picture. Archaic forms such as uncial can also be tried and will enhance children's understanding of how letters are formed if the activity is presented as a form of drawing, perhaps even focusing on the formation of just a small number of letters, rather than as a means of developing neater handwriting. A single line or two of a poem can be chosen for calligraphy and illustration, and these are best chosen by the child, for then they will have a greater sense of commitment to the activity. Faith schools might encourage children to choose a sacred verse or proverb and, if appropriate, write and illustrate it in the manner of Victorian framed texts.

The visual imagery of poetry lends itself to illustration, as do other forms of literature, of course, but the succinctness of poetry can focus children's minds on their affective response. Choosing poetry that fits with a particular time of year and providing an appropriate limited range of colours can produce dramatic drawings; for instance, linking a particular poem to a walk along a tree-lined path on a bright autumn day or reading a poem about winter cold on a frosty morning after a chilly playtime. This is a time when children should be encouraged to draw directly in colour, rather than drawing in graphite pencil and using colour just for the infilling. A brief demonstration could be made by the teacher of drawing bright, overlapping leaf shapes in orange, red and yellow, with the children's attention drawn to conveying colour and pattern, thrill and excitement, the joy of the sunlight and the sensual scrunch of leaves underfoot. Coloured infilling can then be used sparingly where appropriate within the overall design once this is established on the paper.

Children often respond well to drawing or painting in response to music, but it important to be sufficiently au fait with current television advertisements and programmes to ensure that the chosen piece is not well known from this context or the children will draw this. A teacher who did not often watch commercial television once chose 'Morning' from the *Peer Gynt Suite* and was perplexed at the number of cups and saucers drawn by the children; it was currently being used in the advertisement for a well-known brand of coffee! Younger children may find it difficult to distinguish between 'How does it make you feel?' and 'What does it make you think of?', and the former is much more difficult to convey on paper without thinking of the latter. Young children have a stronger desire to create pictures that tell a story than to use drawing to convey moods. For younger children, a cheerful piece, such as Vivaldi's 'Spring' can readily inspire trees in bloom with happy birds flying about, especially if children's attention is directed towards the bird song in the music. The end of the *1812 Overture*, with the bells

Figure 3.3   View from CN Tower, Toronto

ringing, especially the choral version, can be used as an inspiring stimulus for artwork but the children need to know a little of the historical background and to see some pictures of Moscow, including the onion-domed cathedral and churches. Tonal works, such as those by Sibelius, can be paired with Finnish painter, Gallel-Kallela, for drawings and paintings on a cold day, especially if a walk to see a pond in winter can be arranged.

The pairing of Mondrian's *Boogie Woogie* with Joplin's ragtime music also works well and can be linked to the African-American cultural heritage. This can involve looking at maps of Chicago and other large American cities, drawing out grid-like street plans, infilling with squares and rectangles of coloured and textured paper of various thicknesses to suggest buildings of different heights. Photographs taken from the top of a tall building can support this kind of activity, for example, Figure 3.3 shows part of downtown Toronto. British urban children can project their own feelings about their neighbourhoods into images such as Figure 3.3 and discuss the sense of community or dislocation that can be felt in large conurbations. They can be challenged to convey this in their drawings. In Munch's *Scream,* for instance, the artist purposely distorts the human form and chooses his colours to express the pent-up loneliness of his subject.

In all these activities, the pairing of the visual with the musical or poetic image focuses children's attention on thinking about how they feel or might feel, rather than on accurate pictorial representation. They might also be directed to think about the emotional values of colour and tone, the way thick dark lines convey a different emotional message to light wispy lines. The use of examples of abstract subjects by different artists enables children to concentrate on the quality of the lines rather than trying to figure out the story behind the picture. This can then lead into creating their own mood drawings based on just one shape. Mid-Key Stage 2 children (aged 8–10) could, for instance, create a whole series of square 'characters' sitting on a shelf, each in a different mood, using different drawing implements, colours, pressures, tilts of the lines and motifs such as flowers for the love-sick or hankies for the tearful. A similar idea could be used with younger children to encourage visualization of their emotive response to music. The children could create a line of notes sitting on stave lines with different expressions on their 'faces'.

Visualizing and conveying how they feel using graphical media enables children to express their emotional and affective responses without the need to have the words to express them. This can be valuable for children for whom English is not their first language and are, perhaps, also coping with the uncertainties of a new life in a new land and watching trusted adults being confused by it all too. The ability of music to make children *feel*, coupled with another, different non-linguistic means of expressing this feeling can satisfy deep emotional needs. The recognition and objectification of these emotions, the realization that what they feel is common to all people, that artists and musicians understand and can convey these emotions (and even rouse them) can not only be cathartic but deeply comforting. In its use of sublime or metaphorical language, poetry too can speak directly to emotional needs, and the combination of art, music and poetry together can be highly charged and emotionally powerful. It therefore needs handling with care in the classroom. The sharing of emotional responses can be a source of social bonding, developing empathy and delight, but it can also inadvertently be a vehicle for exclusion, embarrassment and even derision.

Provided care is taken not to cause any distress when dealing with emotions, using music and poetry as a stimulus for drawing can enable children to see what particular emotions look like, or to name feelings that they have and give account of their rising. Poems about rage, jealousy and fear can be used as a basis for drawings that the child does not need to acknowledge as their own lived experience, but nevertheless allow for exploration and recognition of these feelings. Pretending to be a character in a poem or responding to music is a safer way of exploring negative emotions than real life and, through children's natural capacity for play, provides them with a new mantle that they can hide under as well as try on. Music is also, of course, a source of joy and a means of escape into a happier world, as poetry can make the heart glad, through rhythm, rhyme and wordplay as well as its subject matter. Drawing in response to songs designed to lift the spirits can promote a deep sense of well-being that is difficult to provide through other means. The stimulation of chemical triggers in the brain that respond to the music, the sound of the words and their metaphorical overtones, and which are then expressed through the non-linguistic channel of drawing, may be providing feedback at a sub-cognitive biological level that contributes to both emotional and physical health.

Much joy can be had in the social music and art-making involved in theatre. This is an opportunity for large-scale drawing for backdrops and scenery, provided that children's roles are not reduced to infilling adult-drawn outlines. Few teachers are great artists and it is infinitely preferable to use children's good ideas and drawings than to colour in weak adult ones. Involvement of all the children can come through commissioning the class to design the backdrop and scenery. Individual sketching of ideas can lead to selection and refining of the best, which can be scaled up and plotted onto large sheets of paper or card. The sense of involvement, empowerment and pride is well worth the effort.

Summary

'Drawing to feel', has explored the affective and emotional dimension of drawings, which inevitably has meant a greater focus on drawings within Art than on other subjects. However, there are links with 'Drawing to design', which focuses not just on inventiveness, but on the ability to match ideas to context and purpose. For this, a perceptive empathy with an intended user is required. Using drawing to portray and develop one's own feelings enhances the ability to consider the feelings, preferences and desires of others. This much needed capacity is not just for the school room but also for life skills that will last a lifetime. Using drawing to make inner feelings visible and able to be examined, considered and, perhaps, even confronted, seems a worthwhile role for this highly adaptable medium. The individual drawing, or a series of drawings, may contain a repeated motif or give evidence of resolution of thoughts, ideas and feelings.

By offering children a wide range of opportunities that can stimulate and elicit creative responses, teachers can contribute towards the growth and development of that ill-defined quality called 'emotional intelligence', the combination of Howard Gardner's (1984) inter- and intra-personal intelligences. Unlike Gardner (2007), however, I would want to argue for a sixth 'new mind' which is a spiritual sense, that the process of drawing can evoke. Deep flow, in Csikszentmihalyi's (2002) sense, is close to a form of meditation as the heart rate slows and consciousness of external distractions diminishes. The journey of inner discovery through drawing in response to an observation, perception, memory or inner image takes on its own momentum and forges its own path. The special circumstances in which these interactive journeys can take place are not always easy to organize in school, perhaps by their very nature they are not able to be 'organized' at all. Perhaps the best that teachers can hope for is to provide the kind of supportive, empathetic environment in which trust is established and risk-taking feels safe. Encouraging children's spiritual development in Howe et al.'s (2001) sense, of encouraging awe and wonder through close observation of the natural as well as of the made world, expressing admiration for the children's own work as well as providing examples of work by established and recognized masters of the field, can create a classroom environment in which those most essential human emotions of all can flourish: happiness, security and a sense of well-being.

Dimension 4

Drawing to see

For the past 700 years, Western culture has placed a high value on achieving a photo-realistic representation of the observed world, both as an artistic genre and for illustrations in the sciences and the humanities. Despite the development of abstract and conceptual art during the past 100 years, 'being able to draw' still means, to many people, the ability to make an accurate representation on paper of the observed world. The development of the techniques for doing so in the early modern period of European history (1400 onwards) was aided by the use of various devices such as screens and grids, and there are extant drawings by Dürer demonstrating just how to use them. Knowledge of the tonal values that we perceive in the observed world enables artists to mimic those perceptions in a way that the viewer can interpret as if seeing the real objects, people or scenes that are represented on the flat surface of the paper or canvas.

The twentieth century saw the development of other ways of representing the world through an explosion of abstract and conceptual artistic movements and, for the first time, children's drawings were valued as art in their own right. Artists such as Klee and Mondrian championed the acceptance of the child's perspective and artistic conventions. They appreciated the freshness and vigour of the untutored eye and hand, and attempted to incorporate these characteristics into their own work. After total war, the innocent eye was needed to remake a world gone bad. The assumption that drawing *comes from the inner life of the child*, untainted by social pressure, became popular as early twentieth-century artists became enamoured with Primitivism, combining sources from so-called 'primitive cultures' and from child art. This confusion can also be seen in the early writers on child art. For instance, Eng (1931) paralleled the development of children's drawings with the art of Palaeolithic hunter-gatherers and contemporary South African Bushmen.

Beneath this search for the quintessential in child art was the idea prevalent across much of the twentieth century. Shiff (1998) calls this a 'cultural mythology' which enabled such juxtapositions, which were especially promoted and popularized through the works of Roger Fry, for whom 'the child ... constitute[ed] a certain literary or rhetorical figure and locus of a grand cultural mythology, a point of condensation for many of the concepts and structures that were enabling European society to negotiate its own modernity' (Shiff, 1998: 158).

That modernity included war and carnage on an unprecedented scale. In stark contrast to the sureties of Victorian technological prowess, which bolstered a sense of moral superiority and inevitable progress, the twentieth century saw the empire-builders destroying each other and themselves. The Victorians had rightly championed the cause of social justice for children on the basis of their vulnerability, but this belief in childhood innocence coloured parts that should have been left alone. The idea that child art arose from some inner well-spring that was (and should be) untainted by the culture with which they were surrounded was mistaken, yet this informed a belief in non-intervention by adults in developing children's drawing skills that often persists today.

The development of child art

Early researchers into the development of children's art frequently asked the child to draw a picture for which no contextual or stylistic cues were given, yet the product was assumed to be typical of the individual child's artistic production and, hence, of 'child art' in general. Assumptions were frequently made about children's drawings without consulting the children. Kellogg (1959), apparently, explicitly instructed her researchers not to ask the child to indicate their intentions or viewpoint on their drawings.

Children's graphic development was assumed to be both *biologically determined* and *teleological*, leading, by the inner unfolding of creativity, towards the accurate representation of observed reality. Luquet (1927) classified children's drawings into four progressive stages:

- fortuitous realism
- failed realism
- intellectual realism
- visual realism.

Such beliefs about how children's drawing skills developed led to the claim that children's intelligence could be measured by the way children drew human figures: the 'Draw-a-Man' test (Goodenough, 1926). The validity of this idea was quickly refuted by other researchers. Eisner

(1972: 199–200) cites an interesting study which casts considerable doubt on this claim: 34 young children were divided randomly into two groups and given the 'Draw-a-Man' test. On four occasions across a two-week period, half of the group were asked to assemble a 14-piece jigsaw of a human figure in which each piece represented a different part of the body. On re-test, this group scored much more highly than the others. Whatever 'Draw-a-Man' tests, observed Eisner, it cannot be intelligence, since four brief sessions could not have made such an impact. Perhaps experience with the jigsaw puzzle interpreted for the children the way they were expected to respond in the test.

In another study cited by Eisner, a researcher who had classified nursery aged children's drawings on a 5-point scale, was able, by discussing their work with them and suggesting 'more advanced possibilities', to move them up a level of the scale. Both these cases seem to illustrate young children's willingness and enthusiasm to learn from an interested and supportive adult. It is almost as if the children said to themselves 'Oh, is that what you wanted me to do!' and did it. In both cases, the positive intervention of the adult provided a model for the learning child.

Underlying the early ideas of progress in children's drawing abilities was a stage-theory view of the child's artistic development (paralleling Piaget's theories in other cognitive areas). Luquet's classifications pervaded much of early thinking about the development of children's art, including Lowenfeld (1947) and Kellogg (1959). These studies viewed the aim of drawing as being the accurate representation of observations of the world and the development of children's drawing abilities as progress towards such 'camera shots' of the world around them. Lowenfeld (1947) listed six stages of development in child art, which he saw as natural aspects of human development through which he thought the child must pass, extrapolated from observations of American children, without realizing the specific cultural influences of time and place as the children tried to produce work that pleased their teacher and conformed to their perceptions of the pictorial norms of their society.

Behind such stage theory schemas of child art development are some unstated and dubious assumptions. First, that children's drawings are rooted in the nature of human cognition and not in the nature of society. Such lack of cultural relativism denies recognition of the social context in which children of all cultures develop their mark-making and misleads teachers into not acknowledging the specific cultural context of children's drawings and artistic output. If drawing development is seen as biologically determined, then children who do not draw in a certain way by a certain age are to be viewed as mentally inferior. If biologically determined, then attainment of the various stages requires no teaching, only opportunity. This is clearly not the case as children who receive little education in art have more limited skill than those who do. The second assumption is that the social functions of drawings (and art in general) in Western society is typical of all human societies and has not changed across time. This becomes unnerving when applied in schools in countries that have very strong but very different artistic traditions, on the assumption that becoming a 'developed nation' requires it.

Finally, this 'stage development' view of child art discounted non-representational artistic output, even as it flowered within twentieth-century Western culture. Some of the best known works of Picasso, Mondrian and Klee would all have failed the tests being applied to assess children's drawing abilities. Seeing the artist as recorder of observable reality, without recognizing the technical tricks employed by trained artists to achieve such renditions, was out of step with mid-twentieth century art, which viewed the artist as communicator of an inner image that relates affectively to its audience, often relying on form, visual symbolism and metaphorical suggestion. Klee's *A Young Lady's Adventure* (1921) uses lines, not to express observed reality, but to explore the dark and shadowy side of the 'adventure' undertaken. Kandinsky combined conventional placement (for example, the triangular arrangement of many Orthodox Madonnas) with abstract shapes to express his view of the essence of art. The mistrust of abstract art in Western society, which persisted throughout much of the twentieth century (and the continued preference given to pictorial art as a model to which children should aspire) has led to the marginalization of other forms of drawing that children can be encouraged to produce, some of which might have more potential for genuine creative development than the production of a 'picture' of something seen, remembered or imagined. That children were more than capable of producing drawings in several genres was not recognized.

Even a brief skim through Matthews's (2002) reflective documentation of his son Ben's artistic output demonstrates the wide range of works produced by one child. Ben's continued fascination with machines and robots is evident throughout. Children's drawings are not separate from the rest of their lives. What they choose to draw for their own pleasure reflects their interests and current obsessions, including television and computer game characters. Matthews's understanding of his son's artistic output in its relationship to his play fantasies is apposite. He observes that children's war drawings (as well as playing) are often overlooked and devalued, yet they deal with 'line of sight, trajectory and moment of impact, and, at a deeper level, justice, heroism and the management of power' (Matthews, 2002: 186).

Hayley's butterfly (Figure 3.1), drawn for her own pleasure, is the kind of image that would please most adults. She was 6 years old when she drew this and shows a developing sense of colour, pattern, symmetry, even whimsy. It too demonstrates the influence of contemporary television culture on child art, whether Disney or other product-themed cartoon shows, such as *Rainbow Brite*, *My Little Pony* or *Little Mermaid*. Piaget has been criticized by social constructivists for seeing the child as lone scientist but it is also true that children are not lone artists. Their imagery and choice of subject matter comes from the social and cultural world that they inhabit and into which they are actively seeking to find their place.

Despite such claims as:

> Unlike adults, children [aged 6–10] cannot choose which style to draw in ... Children are unable to choose how to express mood, either by colour or line ... Drawings are produced by accident ... they see no alternatives in how to draw and are completely oblivious to alternatives ... Their work manages to charm adults, but to see them as artists is naive. (Winner, 1982: 23)

In fact, children can learn and utilize a whole range of genres and drawing styles. Figure 4.1 shows a self-portrait in the style of Paul Klee by 7-year-old Glen. Since the introduction of the National Curriculum for Art and Design in the UK, children have been shown examples of a much wider range of artistic genres than at any time in British educational history, potentially changing their picture-making and designing skills. This introduction to many varied styles of art and drawing could help children to be more flexible about their graphic productions and enable them to be more willing to try out several designs based on different drawing styles. Glen's class were experimenting with making portraits in the styles of several artists. Klee's work had struck a chord with Glen, enabling him to produce a visually satisfying piece that demonstrates that Year 3 children are quite capable of 'drawing or painting in the style of' a particular artist. The sophistication of being able to take on board a totally new style of drawing and make it your own and produce a pleasing work of art in the course of two hours is within the capability of an ordinary 7-year-old. Glen was equally at home across a range of genres including pattern-making, cartoons, and labelled diagrams for science.

Such work shows that children's drawing skills are far more fluid and adaptable than was once thought. It also means that exposure to different drawing genres can enable children to access and exploit these appropriately for different situations. Wilson (1992) discovered that children from an Egyptian village with few outside influences had a more restricted visual vocabulary and showed far less diversity in their drawings than those of Western culture, where the influence

Figure 4.1   Glen's (age 7) self-portrait in the style of Paul Klee

of television and especially cartoons influenced drawing style. He argued, therefore, that children's art is not inherently creative and untainted but that it is directly influenced by the culture in which the child is growing up.

Children function as part of a multilayered socio-cultural system (Rogoff, 1996) as learners, peers and teachers; as transmitters of culture to each other as well as receivers of culture from older children and adults. They are actively seeking competence and identity within the overlapping and interacting cultural milieux they inhabit. Mental processes cannot be separated from emotional, social and motivational processes. The effort that some researchers have put into finding examples of the onset of various abilities or skills at younger ages than those claimed by Piaget, Lowenfeld and others who hold the stage theory view, suggests that skills are seen as 'mental objects', as if they were contained in the child and not culturally shared. Rogoff (1996) viewed it as preferable if researchers would aim to understand children's changing roles as they participate in communities of thinkers. This implies that child art and drawing capabilities should be seen from a different more socially orientated viewpoint. Children are actively learning from each other and the surrounding adult culture rather than by responding to intrinsic or individual sources. Due credence needs to be given to the cultural influences and expectations on children's drawings.

Children's drawing skills, like all aspects of child development, are far more fluid and adaptable than was once thought but if children are to access and utilize the many genres of drawing, then they need to be shown how. However, it must also be said that while recognizing the limitations of these art development schema, the greatest contribution of these early researchers was to establish that the difference between child and adult art is not just lack of teaching, but also resides in the perceptual and cognitive make-up of children as they mature, as well as in their physical development.

Luquet (1927) claimed that young children draw from an internal model rather than from the external reality that they are seeing. There was some overlap in Luquet's findings with the observations and views of Piaget, who saw the child at this age as having an egocentric rather than exo-centric view of the world (perhaps 'self-centric' would be a better English rendering of Piaget's meaning). The young child is establishing a perspective of the external world from their own position, discovering and creating their place in the world while internalizing its features. For the child, this priority overrides other concerns but does not necessarily mean that this is all the child can do.

Canonical drawing

One of the phenomena identified by Luquet in children was the production of stereotypical images or 'canonical' drawings by children aged

4–6 years. 'Canonical' means being part of an existing canon, a set pattern. It is not quite the same as 'stereotypical' or 'idealized', although both those words are implied. Canonical drawing was one of those phenomena that was later asserted to be evidence of young children's Piagetian self-centric view of the world. However, there were contradictions between the theoretical framework and the findings, which remained largely unresolved.

In the 1970s and 1980s there was a bevy of interest in the fact that young children aged 4–6 years did not draw what they were shown but what they knew about the objects they were shown. The lack of locational realism (drawing what they see) in Key Stage 1 children's drawings may simply be due to the tendency that they more frequently draw from memory or imagination than from direct observation. To apply criteria of realistic representation to the production of an image that has come from the child's head is, therefore, more than a little unfair. Most adults would perform poorly if asked to draw even a quite familiar object from memory. The speed camera sign, for instance, is an important and common sight that most adults struggle to reproduce on paper accurately from memory when asked.

However, Luquet's observation that the child draws from an inner model was explored and it was discovered that many children appeared to have the same internal model. For instance, in accordance with Luquet's stage of 'intellectual realism' from ages 4/5–9 years, Freeman (1980) found that children below age 8 drew cups with handles even if shown a cup that was held with the handle hidden from the child's viewpoint. Younger children produced drawings that emphasized known facts about the object (cups have handles, so should be shown as such) whereas older children produced drawings that showed the object from the child's specific viewpoint, with handle not drawn if they could not see it.

Logically, this appears to contradict the Piagetian framework that children start from their own viewpoint and only later create powerful generalizations about the world, since under that schema, it would be expected that older rather than younger children would depict conservational properties such as cups always having handles even if they cannot themselves see them. Further, it is in direct conflict with the claims made as a result of Piaget's findings in his 'Three Mountains' test in which children assigned their own viewpoint to the teddy bear seated at the opposite side of the table. Surely, if children were self-centric at a young age, they would draw their view of the cups, not an abstracted vision of 'cupness' in order to make it clear that the object is a cup not a bowl?

The phenomenon of canonical drawing prompted considerable debate, such as:

- Were the results due to the young child being more concerned to depict what an object *is* rather than how it *looks* at the moment?
- Was it because young children are rarely asked to draw anything from a specific viewpoint and so have had no practice at what they were being asked to do.

Discussions with children seemed to indicate that they were aware that the handle could not be seen but they had, nevertheless, drawn it showing.

Cox (1992) reported the variations that other researchers devised in order to investigate the phenomenon. For instance, seeing two cups in different orientation appeared to make the children realize that orientation was important. However, my own experiments (Hope, 2003) involving about 200 4–6-year-olds indicated that this did not make any difference, especially with younger children in the age group. Previous studies seemed to suggest that telling the children the object was a cup before they drew it was more likely to lead to canonical drawings. This seems likely, since my children saw both cups with both handles visible at first presentation. They were then asked to draw them again after I had turned one cup so that its handle was hidden, so they knew that both objects were cups. However, one group of 4-year-olds, who were shown the cup in 'handle hidden' position first and to whom I did not name the object but simply invited them to 'draw what you can see', either drew a picture of the snow scene that was on the cup but not the cup itself or a picture suggested to them by the picture on the cup (Figure 4.2).

It was as if they had mentally added the words 'on the cup' to my instructions. Perhaps, in line with Donaldson's (1979) criticisms of Piaget, there is a language problem here and all that these studies show is that the researcher has, to varying degrees, failed to communicate to the children what it is they want them to do. Cox concluded that children do canonicals if there is no reason to do otherwise or if a realistic drawing will lead to object ambiguity. This does not, however, address the reasons why.

One of the problems with the studies quoted by Cox is the small number of children (typically 30) involved in each. Building a theory on such small samples not only falls short on statistical reliability standards but also precluded the researchers from developing a valid theory of what was really going on. Analysing my much larger sample (200+) led me to the belief that canonical drawings are not some quirk of early childhood, but evidence of essential cognitive development. Children close to their fifth birthday most often produce object-centred (canonical) drawings. By age 6, most children produced viewer-centred (locational) drawings. Children who do not produce canonical drawings

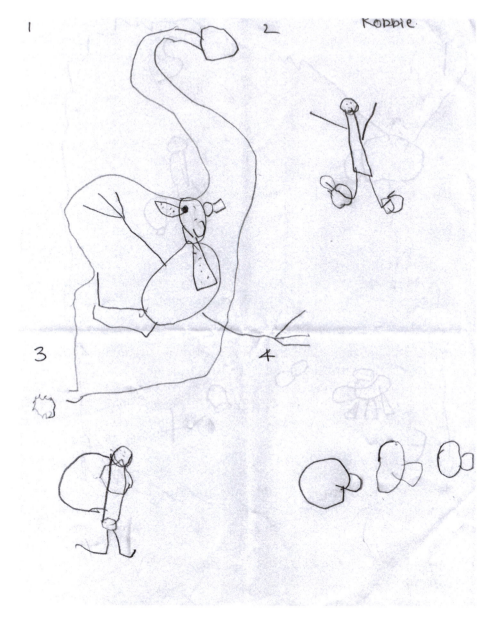

Figure 4.2   'Draw what you see!'

within this 4–6-year-old age band are likely to have developmental language difficulties.

There appear to be parallels with Donaldson's (1992) account of 6-year-old children who were told a story in which characters entered a house and, after each character left again, the children were asked 'Who is still in the house?' When all the characters were gone, the children started inventing new characters, including their friends and family. Donaldson insightfully concluded that the children did not understand that they were being asked to solve 'this problem and this problem only' as defined by the rules stated at the start of the game. This fluidity of young children's thinking enables them to be extremely quick and highly imaginative learners, but it also explains many of their misunderstandings when asked to perform tightly defined tasks designed by adults, including the canonical cups problem.

Children's syntactical understanding before age 7 is insufficiently acute to fully understand the formal difference between the definite articles *the/this/that/those* and the indefinite articles *a/any/some*. Being unable to distinguish these subtleties of the language (which the adult regards as highly apposite) means that a child will produce a drawing of *a tree* whether sitting facing an oak or a pine.

The naming of the object significantly affects the results of the canonical cups problem because children believed they were being asked to draw '*a cup*' not '*this thing you see*'. If the teacher stands holding her coffee cup after playtime and waves it to indicate what is required, the children will draw a canonical cup (*a cup*). If, once they have done that, the teacher turns the cup so the handle is not visible and says, 'Now look really hard and draw this cup as you see it and draw only those bits that you can actually *see* and *not* the bits hidden from your view', most of the class will do as asked. They have drawn *this cup*, not a generalized cup which they can produce from an inner image stored in their memory.

The object involved is just too familiar. Five- to six-year-old children will attempt locational drawings of less familiar forms, for instance, a cup with two handles or a Chinese lidded cup with a leaf strainer. The unfamiliarity of the form makes them look, not just draw from knowledge, memory and imagination. However, they still want to draw the object from what they regard as 'best view', but so too do adults. The desire to solve the problems of capturing line, angle, shadow and so on of a jumble of objects (a pot full of pencils and scissors, for instance) is the kind of problem that artists set themselves, not what the general population does when asked to draw something. Asking a group of adults to draw 'a house', for instance, will result in a set of upmarket canonicals. Canonical drawing is not a stage children pass through which then disappears as other forms take over. It is an attainment that stays with them for life, firmly establishing itself in the child's graphic repertoire. The difference is that adults and older children have the knowledge, experience and capability with language to identify when something else is being expected and will then produce a different response.

At age 5–6 years, there are two sorts of children who do not fall into the trap of drawing 'best view' of the mug, the teddy bear, the chair or whatever it is they are being shown from a strange angle. The more sophisticated see it as a party trick, *'Can you put this strange view onto paper?'* For example, when her class were shown two cups, one with the handle showing and one hidden, Hayley, who drew the beautifully patterned butterfly shown in Figure 3.1, shouted out 'It's no handle. You have to do one with no handle!' but she was ignored, even by her best friend Zara who was sitting beside her. This is firm evidence that the rest of the class fully believed that what they were doing was correct. There were no epiphanies in which children hastily erased their first attempt in the light of Hayley's revelation.

The other group of children who produce locational drawings of familiar objects at a young age are those who have developmental language difficulties. For example, Andy at age 6 drew the back view of a rocking chair, shown in Figure 4.3, His 'map' drawn at age 4 is discussed in 'Dimension 2: Drawing to mean'.

Andy was one of the few children who could use drawing to record his design ideas by the end of Year 1 (Figure 4.4, annotated in discussion with Andy at the time of drawing to record intended materials and construction details). As a non-writer, Andy was still using picturing to place-hold stories beyond the end of Year 1 and this probably helped his designing skills since he thought visually as first choice. By the time he had discussed his ideas, he was able to make a model of the house from a box, which included the yellow door with a split handle.

However, this prowess did not continue as he got older. By age 7 years, other children in his class were easily able to use drawing to develop design ideas, whereas Andy's ability remained static. For instance, while other children confidently used drawing to develop ideas for creating a travel bag for the class mascot, Andy simply drew a bag on a sheet of paper, cut it out and presented it as finished. He was now performing at the same level as the least capable members of the class.

A similar case was an autistic child called Nadia, studied by Selfe (1985), who had exceptional drawing skills as a young child, but ceased to produce these drawings once she started to speak. At age 13 she started to produce canonical drawings. She had started to make generalizations about the world around her and her drawings were evidence of this cognitive progress. Likewise, the accuracy of Andy's drawing is probably due to the limitations of his verbal labelling skills. When such children draw what they are shown, they record the shapes and angles of the scene that they see before them, without accessing a verbally labelled inner schema of this class of objects stored in memory and accessible through a linguistically supported imagination.

Figure 4.3   Andy's drawing of the back of a rocking chair

Canonical drawings, therefore, are not a cutesy aberration of children's drawings which they will eventually outgrow, but evidence of the development of symbolic thinking expressed through graphic representation. As part of their normal development, children come to understand that symbols are cut free from the concrete experience, that names of things are not part of the thing and can be used and manipulated in their own right. This becomes true too for graphic imagery.

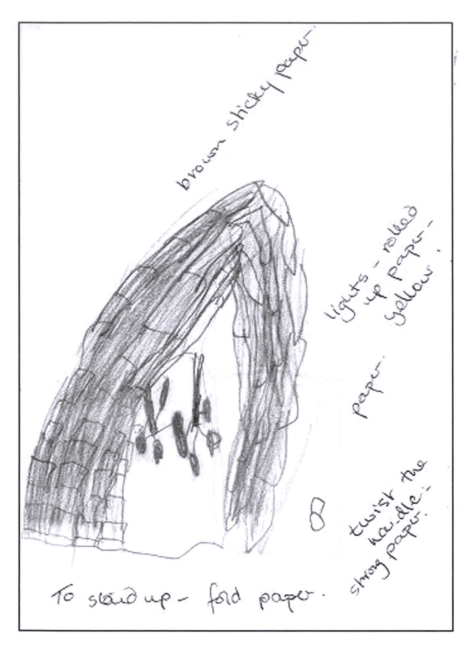

brown sticky paper

lights – rolled
up paper –
yellow.

paper

twist the
handle..

To stand up – fold paper.

strong paper.

Figure 4.4   Andy's design drawing of a model of a house for a story character

Canonical drawings represent the child's inner visual image which accompanies classification of the world around them. Shown a familiar object, such as a cup, they draw the cup the way that they know a cup should be, not the odd view in front of them. When shown an unfamiliar object, they draw what they see as accurately as they are able. A child who has not classified all instances of cups, chairs and other common objects in their environment as specific instances of classes of these objects, and internalized this generalization sufficiently to produce a canonical drawing of them with reasonable competence by age 5, will probably show signs of language difficulty or will have prompted adult concerns in some other way. Canonical drawings are graphic symbols that represent all instances of a particular class: a house, a girl, a rainbow, and so on. As children move on into producing locational drawings (this cup from this angle with that part of the pattern showing) they have begun to use their inner images as if they were a language whose syntax can be changed and adapted for a range of purposes. This involves conscious exploitation and manipulation of the symbol system: graphic meta-cognition.

The ability to use drawing to design something new, rather than make an accurate observational drawing of what is seen, requires the ability to manipulate inner imagery. It also requires the ability to marry this to language. Andy (discussed above) did not become a good designer. Although at age 6 he could draw what he would like to make and say what he would make it from (Figure 4.3), which seemed promising, by age 9 years his classmates had far overtaken him in the ability to use drawing for designing. While he stayed at the stage of being able to draw what he would like to make, they moved on to labelling, discussing, adapting, re-drafting their ideas, and so on, in which his difficulties in generative language hampered him from becoming a participant.

One reason why canonical drawings are essential for designing is that drawings made from observation show the defects and idiosyncrasies of the specific object that is being drawn, whereas the canonical drawing reflects the generalized inner image that is essential for drawing from the imagination. By making a sketch of what is in the mind's eye, the designer converts the mental image into a visual image that loses the disadvantages of the ephemeral nature of the mental image while still being fluid enough to be re-interpreted by the eye and manipulated by the brain.

'How to draw' books

These books of 'How to draw Horses … Cats … Cartoons … Dinosaurs' and so on are available in bookshops worldwide, in places as far apart as Toronto, Paris, London and Batu Pahat in southern Malaysia. Looking at the series of images of the stages towards a final drawing, it is clear that what is being taught is how to produce a standardized canonical drawing by an adult. An adult's stylized drawing of a lion or a cow is being substituted for the child's own schema that they have developed and internalized. The instructional images base the drawings on a series of ellipses or circles of different sizes and positions, which the child should copy in exactly the same size and position as the model. The written instructions stress the importance of getting these initial shapes right.

The final products of the process are mostly profiles with all the salient parts showing, as canonical drawings always do. The tiger, for instance, facing right, stands with all four legs showing and its tail curved out behind, its stripes regularly spaced down its back and a suitably fierce open mouth. It is not crouching, rolling, scratching or performing any of the many actions that real tigers do. The turtle is frequently drawn in a similar way to most 6–7-year-olds' canonical turtle, except that it lacks the smile that most children add. This turtle will not be eating or swimming. If it were to have one leg in the air it would be the front one, as if walking, not a back one extended behind to assist cooling the underbelly, which would be more typical of real turtle behaviour.

'How to draw a cat' is not the same as how to draw a tabby cat stretched out across the windowsill with a wonderful view of the Scilly Isles behind or looking dark and fiercesome with the storm clouds gathering (in the manner of local artist Patsy Swanborough). There are many children's books about cats with wonderful evocative illustrations of cats in all their moods, positions and activities. If models of 'How to draw a cat' are to be shown to children, then such models abound in high-quality children's literature: *Ginger* by C. Voake (1997), or *The Patchwork Cat* by Fournoy (1985), for instance, are frequently to be found in Key Stage 1 classrooms. Teachers of older children could use these as resources for drawing, discussing the way in which the artist has captured the mood, the pose or the movement of the cat. If a real cat cannot be brought in for children to observe and draw, then a video of a cat playing, running, jumping, sleeping and being stroked and petted is essential if realistic drawings of a cat are intended as the result of the activity. A series of initial sketches from life could be drawn and used as the basis of a Cubist cat, for instance. This would extend children's visual vocabulary and enable them to create a final product that did not depend for final effect on the ability to produce either stylized canonicals or photo-realism, both of which are equally inappropriate aims for Key Stage 2 children.

The key problem with the 'How to draw' books is that they are circumventing the very problem that the average child over the age of 7 is grappling with: how to draw *this* cat, or *that* tiger in the grass, or even *my* house or *my* mum. Not 'a woman' of uncertain age, race and disposition, but their own mother as they so intimately know her. The child is trying to move away from canonical representation into a form of drawing that captures the essence of observation in a new and more satisfying way. The Key Stage 2 child is searching for a new way of constructing their observations of the world and looking for new schemas which will enable them to break out from the generalization that served them so well in constructing sophisticated mental models and supporting the development of language structure and syntax. The dissatisfaction with their drawing output (often from about age 7 onwards) is due to its comparison with an increasing range of inner images for the same category of objects, or by judging someone else's representation of the object to be better than their own. The child's criteria by which they judge their own canonicals is changing; substituting new canonicals for old does not help.

Caricatures, cartoons and animations

As a genre, cartoons are often derided, both as poor literature and poor art, probably because they successfully extract features of each to create a genre which lies somewhere between the two. The cultural snobbery of those who felt all great art is 'pure' and should be 'high' gave cartoons a difficult path into acceptability and created barriers that have still to be completely crossed. This overspills into what is considered acceptable to be taught to children and devalues an art form that children enjoy, relate to, forms part of their day-to-day lives and which can form, either directly or indirectly, a stimulus for children's own work. This viewpoint still persists, despite Lichtenstein's works now hanging in galleries in the USA and Europe, which used the cartoon style of the period to powerfully criticize the trivialization of the carnage of the Second World War.

Little analysis of the skills required to read the pictorial text was undertaken until recently (Rosen, 1996) and so these powerful forms of graphic storytelling remained unrecognized and underused as a way of developing children's literacy or graphicacy within the school setting. As Rosen (1996) explains, graphic stories demand the ability to read the developing plot at several levels simultaneously, to decode and remember quite small graphic details that are significant later for development of the plot. Cartoons (both static and animated forms) often exploit changes of facial expression in order to convey information about voice and mood, and so carry the storyline along in a single pen stroke. Children learn to interpret these visual clues and are able to follow the thoughts and feelings of the characters as the story unfolds, often with little recourse to language. Sometimes quite subtle visual clues in one frame are left hanging until a much later stage in the story, when a correct interpretation and memory of them is needed to understand the motives and subsequent actions of the characters. These can be emotionally powerful stories, told with the minimum of words, and that do not depend on the child's ability to read text for their enjoyment.

As a free-choice activity, both at home and in school, children often draw their favourite cartoon or television characters. Some children practise drawing specific characters over and over again until they have perfected the form to a point at which they become actively admired by their friends for their skill. This should be encouraged rather than ignored. Children who can reproduce and adapt a drawn image with this degree of skill, not to say persistence, are displaying a high level of graphic capability. Too frequently such capability is ignored by adults because the subject matter is considered unworthy, rather than considering that the dedication of that amount of time on perfecting the skill should be commended. Even as they master the genre of comics and manga, children will adapt and subvert it in the same way as they do when role-playing the characters.

For Key Stage 2 children, especially those who are beginning to despair of their ability to reproduce the observed world on paper, manga and other graphic literature can be used as source materials and stimulus to draw, even if this means direct copying or even tracing. Tracing provides the child with a realistic outline which they can then colour and feel satisfied with their achievement. It also allows them to experience through their fingers the path that their pencil needs to take in order to produce a particular shape on the paper that represents the object or human in a particular pose. The plotting of the shape, the establishing of the loci of points by the hand is translated into a neural pathway that makes the child more likely to be able to produce the same shape away from the tracing. Adults who wish to decry all forms of tracing should attempt to copy a picture before and after tracing it, and observe their greater accuracy after the trace.

The same principle applies to copying the work of those who have already mastered effective rendering of the human body. Manga and graphic stories provide a popular and readily available source of demonstration materials on how to draw the human body in a range of poses in a context that is popular with the children. For instance, these works can be used for children's research into how changes in facial expressions can be represented, or how figures can be shown as running, squatting, kneeling. Because the figures are shown in just a few lines, children can see how a particular artist has chosen to represent a character in a particular pose. Children frequently are able to reproduce the characters of cartoon and video media in perfect proportional representation, while their ability to draw other objects or people from life demonstrates only a rudimentary grasp of this skill.

Accessible, contemporary and child-friendly graphic genres such as manga should be part of the visual world to which children are introduced. Instead of discouraging these drawings as somehow unworthy of the name of art, children can be encouraged to be creative with the scenes and characters. They can begin to play with characterization, pose, foreshortening and other artistic devices within a less challenging graphic context than drawing from observation of real life. They will, in fact, be following in the footsteps of artists' apprentices worldwide. The workshops of Renaissance masters were full of young men who traced and copied the drawings of their masters. Titian had so many of these employees that his patrons complained that the only part of the painting that was his was the initial sketch and the final details. The many paintings hanging in galleries with the tag 'in the style of' or 'from the workshop of' are testimony to the high level of skill demonstrated by these unknown tracers and copyists. Some of them became known artists in their own right and some became the recognized grand masters of the genre (Leonardo da Vinci, Michelangelo).

Observational drawing

Observational drawing requires the child to relate their drawing activity to the world in a new way. In order to engage in locational observational drawing, the child needs to understand that what is being asked of them is to represent the particular object in front of them, not any object of this class. Instead of drawing an internalized image that represents the essential features of that particular class of objects, perhaps with some variations of pose or detailing, the child is now being asked to produce a drawing that represents *this* bird, not *any* bird; *that* house, not *a* house.

It is often said that learning to make good observational drawings depends on learning to look. A prerequisite of this is understanding the kind of looking that is being demanded. Focusing the children's attention on the specific features of the object, discussing these at some length and even talking about how these could be rendered in the chosen medium helps the children to understand the purpose of the activity and, therefore, increases the likelihood of success. This discussion must include a realistic appraisal of what is possible with the materials provided. Key Stage 2 children might try a range of media for initial drawings, leading into a choice of the one that best suits the way they will choose to represent the object in a final piece. After the initial trials, they should be able to discuss the advantages and disadvantages of each medium. This will not only enable children to make the best choice for the way that they wish to represent the object but also help them to understand that each medium has its limitations as well as its advantages. Their inability to draw well with one medium may be because it is less well suited to the task in hand, or to the current maturity of their hand muscles or their previous inexperience with the medium in this context. All drawing involves making compromises. Children need to feel empowered to make choices about which compromises they will make: colour, level of detail, texture, and so on.

As children move through Key Stage 2, they may become increasingly dissatisfied with their graphic output. Instead of comparing what they have drawn to what they hold in memory or imagination, they begin to compare what they have drawn with the reality of their observations. Not surprisingly, the image falls short. When they compare their work with that of older children, they can see that the older child has captured a sense of the object onto the page in a way that they cannot yet manage. Their perception of the world is changing rapidly and their mastery of graphic representation cannot keep pace. They are dissatisfied with their own performance and, unless inspired to persist, will quickly lose heart. This is exacerbated by only showing children artistic works that exploit single point perspective, and thereby imply that there is only one way of looking.

For instance, the children in a Year 3 class were shown work by Klee, Picasso, Francis Bacon and Giacometti (Figure 4.1 is one of the drawings made in this series). Their teacher discussed with them how the different artists used different styles and techniques to convey different aspects of the human body or face. The children were encouraged to try drawing in different styles and with different materials. They understood that these choices could be used to convey different moods and messages about a person's character or circumstances. Based on a study of Giacometti's sulptural figures, the children worked in pairs and bent each other into interesting poses and drew pin-men to record the positions of the limbs. From this followed the making of wire frame models that could still be moved and bent until the child was happy with the final pose before the limbs of the little figures were wrapped in plaster-impregnated cloth.

By focusing the children's attention solely on the shape of the body and insisting that they used single lines for the positions of the limbs, to match the wire from which the models would be made, the teacher enabled all the children to produce pleasing results. That the models were not in the same proportions as a 'real' human body was not important; neither were Giacometti's. An appropriate drawing genre had been used for the task and the children's confidence and visual vocabulary was enhanced.

Learning to look

Looking through drawing prolongs the looking. (Rubens and Newland, 1989: 15)

This kind of looking creates a very different relationship between viewer and object than does ordinary looking. Looking in order to draw requires that the spatial relationship between each of the parts of the object be correctly observed. The numbers of parts, their angle, relative size and shape, their texture and tone, whether they are in sunlight or shadow, all these things must be noted, even if the final representation of them falls short of that hoped for. Observing something closely for a long time, in order to represent it by drawing, imprints the object or land-scape on the memory in a very intense way and the details of the scene can be recalled long after. The concentration and attention to detail required for this means that every aspect of the object is examined and considered. Holiday sketches create a far deeper memory of the place than do holiday photographs.

However, an observational drawing is not just an exact copying, as can be judged by the frequency or infrequency with which an adult artist looks at the object as they draw. When the drawing begins, a great deal of attention is paid to the object or view. Getting the positions, angles and scale of the objects is the first consideration. Once this is done, then details are added, and the artist looks at the object less frequently because they are engaged in creating a pleasing drawing. It is only in moments of uncertainty that a glance will again be given to the object. Observations of children engaged in successful observational drawing suggest that similar patterns of activity occur. Where children are being less successful, the pattern of activity is very different. For instance, they may rush into drawing the main object in the view without considering how they will fit in other parts of the drawing at the same scale. Looking through a clear plastic viewing grid and having a grid lightly pencilled onto the drawing paper will help children with the placing of objects, as it does for adults.

Level of detail
Children are less adept than adults at adjusting the level of detail required according to the context (Van Sommers, 1984). For instance, children may busy themselves drawing fashion details such as pockets

and zips on a design for a puppet, which could not be made with the materials in the tray in front of them on the table, only to redraw the details onto card and stick fabric over the top, thus hiding the drawing completely.

Knowing the level of detail required to be drawn for a given purpose is a skill that develops with practice as well as with maturity. Judging the salient features needed to render an appropriate representation of the object in view is a finely tuned capability. Both children and unpractised adults may try to draw in every brick on a house front and every tile on its roof. The experienced artist, on the other hand, uses a few lines to suggest this infill and allows the paper to speak for the rest, secure in the knowledge that the human eye and experience of buildings will know that this device indicates that the whole surface is to be read as having this pattern. Knowing how much of such detail to put in is part of the development of the artistic know-how, as is the knowledge that the object of the activity is as much to do with creating a pleasing and well-balanced picture as with rendering observational accuracy.

Children can be helped to begin to understand this balance, although they will struggle to achieve it during their primary school years, by being given the opportunity to examine drawings and watercolours by masters in the field. They should be shown the work of a wide range of artists, including works that they can themselves emulate. Looking at landscapes, for instance, they may be fascinated to compare Turner's on-the-spot sketches with his final portrayal (and notice the significant changes that he made to some of the scenes), but also look at a wide range of modern artists' renditions of local landmarks (children in Cornwall could look at the works of the St Ives school of painters). Looking at the works of a range of artists help children to realize, not only that different painters employed very different styles, but also that they worked at different levels of detail. Showing children works such as those of the pre-Raphaelites or Dürer's *Praying Hands*, may evoke a sense of awe at the level of detail portrayed, but using David Hockney or Mattisse for inspiration may be a more realistic model for children in the 8–10 years age group.

Texture, tone, shading and shadows

Children of all ages can explore texture through experimenting with different surfaces, materials and equipment. This experimental work is best done through focusing on creating patterns, rather than immediately incorporating techniques into observational drawings. Children need time to build up a repertoire and visual vocabulary before being able to apply this knowledge in a more challenging application. They can discover how to make different textured patterns through using the same media in different ways, perhaps through using a stick of chalk on its side as well as drawing with the end, or discover the many different effects that can be made with an ordinary graphite pencil. A range of pencils, from HB through to 8B enables children to create texture and shading that enable the more convincing representation of an object. Children in Key Stage 2 need to be taught and encouraged to use different grips when using these pencils, so that the side of the lead as well as the point can be used effectively.

Children find shading and shadows to indicate direction of light difficult, even at age 11 years. A soft pencil (6B or above) can be rolled on its side to produce a realistic shadow fairly easily and children in upper Key Stage 2 (age 9–11) can learn to develop this skill. Younger children rarely show shadows and find them difficult to portray. This is even more problematic in coloured drawings, especially when using a pen, than when using a pencil. Shadows locate an object on its ground, so in terms of achieving locational realism, it is absolutely vital to success. The use of putty rubbers or ordinary soft rubbers cut into fine points to blur edges and improve shading as well as draw in details on shaded sides of objects, can be taught to older and more able children in the final years of primary school. Before this age, children see rubbers merely as correction tools, unless they have regularly seen adults using them for drawing.

Experiments in tone can begin in Year 3 (age 7–8). This can begin from a comparative study of artists who use very different tonal ranges within the same genre. Looking at how different artists have represented trees, for instance, makes a fascinating study, including Cezanne's *The Great Pine* and Mondrian's *The Grey Tree*. By looking closely at the tones of the colours employed, children can see how the effects have been created. Such study is an important part of children's visual education.

Genres within observational drawing

Generally speaking, children are expected to learn to recognize and use different kinds of drawing on request, without the kind of drawing they are expected to use being made clear. In a history drawing, for example, an element of emotive suggestion may be appropriate, whereas for science, recording observations in dispassionate, objective terms is required. When children are too young to distinguish between a science and a history lesson, then to expect the correct form of drawing genre is plainly unrealistic. However, as children get older, they can begin to distinguish different forms for different purposes. By the end of their primary years, they have become efficient users of a range of observational forms. They achieve this by being sophisticated readers of the world and through developing finely tuned capacities for sorting and classifying the demands of the social and educational world. Their ability to read other people's meanings and intentions and to relate this to prior experience enables them to judge the kinds of drawing appropriate for each situation.

The learning of these conventions, and knowing how and when to use them is a sophisticated process to which too little attention is given. Children need guidance as to the conventions appropriate for different situations and purposes. If they are simply told to 'draw a picture' then they will be unsure which convention is being asked for. Not surprisingly, therefore, they frequently opt for the stylized stereotype that conforms to no specific drawing genre except that of 'children's drawings'.

Developing children's understanding and capabilities within observational drawing requires clarity on the part of the teacher of the kind of drawing that is expected and some indication and instruction on its conventions as determined by the purpose of the drawing.

Example 1: still life

This includes both living and non-living objects that do not move and are situated within a relatively enclosed space or similarly non-moving environment, such as flowers, fruit or other plant materials in a vase or dish or on a table, usually with the intent that children will produce a product that comes under the heading of 'Art'.

These objects are usually specifically arranged for the purpose, rather than being as found, and artists frequently spend more time arranging the objects than drawing them, trying out different arrangements of the objects, backcloths, vases and other supporting props, as well as experimenting with the light levels, direction and angle of sunlight or artificial light, and, of course, their own viewpoint.

When asking children to draw a group of objects, it is important that they too have this level of involvement with the subject prior to drawing. It is essential, not just for creating a pleasing arrangement, but also for the level of involvement and first-hand experience of the objects themselves. If children are to draw plant materials, they should choose the flowers and arrange them in the vase, or the fruit on the dish. In this way, they know the components of the subject before beginning to draw, through touch and smell, and have a strong sense of the spatial arrangement of the objects, through handling and arranging, which starts to build the picture within the child's head.

Such full and intimate knowledge is essential for good observational drawing. Through handling the components, the children become more deeply aware of their physical size and volume. As well as their form and colour, they know their weight, texture, malleability and their smell. This last is important for any good drawing because the smell of an object so often produces an emotional reaction. Flowers are enjoyed for their scent as much as for their appearance. Fruit or other foodstuffs are appetizing because of their aroma, in both raw and cooked forms. This pleasure in the tactile and aromatic qualities of the subject will convey itself in the process of drawing.

Example 2: analytical drawings

The drawing of human-made objects can be required in History, RE, Geography, Science or Design and Technology. The child is usually expected to ignore the background, which is often simply their ordinary working table or a box in which the object is placed. The children are expected to produce a realistic likeness of the object, with essential features in correct proportions with regard to each other. A simple line drawing may be expected, with minimum shading or textural detail, unless this is an obviously distinguishing feature of the object. The children's expertise in producing canonical drawings is required here, to be able to decide which are the essential salient features of the object that need recording, in order to identify it as a particular class of object. This may prove difficult if it is the first object of its kind that the children have seen, but they will nevertheless know that what is being expected of them is to produce a drawing of the object in such a way as to portray it in the best view of its most salient and distinguishing features.

A sub-genre within this kind of observational drawing is the scientific drawing. This is an abstraction of what is of importance for the scientific purpose, which is to be rendered in greater clarity than other features, some of which may be highly relevant to the working of the device being depicted, yet are deemed irrelevant to the drawing. A drawing of the equipment used to collect rain does not require raindrops to be shown entering the funnel, for instance. By the beginning of Key Stage 2, many children will be familiar with cut-away diagrams and may be able to produce these themselves for familiar objects. They will also, by this age, be familiar with the expectation that such things should be drawn in relation to an imaginary baseline horizontal to the bottom edge of the page.

Younger children do not necessarily make this assumption, as their drawings of such scenes as trees around a pond, all sprouting from the circular pond, but in different directions with regard to the adult's expected lower baseline. Children playing ring-a-roses or other circle games will also be portrayed in this fashion, and researchers into children's drawings have seen these as failed attempts to draw 'realistically'. This lack of knowledge about expectations of such conventions has led to some odd conclusions about children's scientific knowledge. For instance, presenting 5–6-year-old children with a sheet of line drawings of cut-away bottles all at different angles and asking them to draw the level of the water if each bottle is half full will produce some curious results, even if a half-full clear plastic bottle is used as a demonstration. Most children will have drawn the level of the water parallel to the top of the bottle, even when they can clearly see that the water in the demonstration bottle is not, unless the adult conducting the experiment asks them to verbalize their observations before drawing the line that represents the water level.

Looking carefully at some children's drawings may reveal that they have attempted to draw the water splashing about inside the bottle as it turns, rather than draw the level once the water has subsided. These results indicate that what is being shown is not related to the children's observational capabilities nor to their scientific knowledge, but to their understanding of the verbal instructions and the conventions of scientific drawings to which they are not privy through having been considered too young to have been taught them prior to the experiment into their capabilities.

The introduction of non-fiction texts in Key Stage 1 through the National Literacy Strategy has meant that children are exposed to such conventions at an earlier age than was previously the case, and so they are able to produce labelled diagrams at a much younger age than before. This includes conventions such as arrows, legends and keys, and shading to indicate different parts of an object or creature. This has provided children with another way of using drawing to model and communicate their ideas. It can also mean that children become less anxious about the realistic accuracy of their drawing, 'You can see what it's meant to be because it's got a label on', and use an interactive mix of writing and graphics with some confidence.

Summary

Exploring the dimension of 'Drawing to see' has taken a wider view of this use of drawing than simply the production of lifelike images, realistic containers of static observations, the kind of expectations against which children's drawings were measured in past times. Since the early days of research into children's artistic output, the world of art itself has changed. 'Seeing' from an artistic point of view is no longer considered to be a means of recording observations, a form that dominated Western art between the rise of humanism and the invention of the photographic camera. 'Seeing' within art has become closer to Wittgenstein's 'seeing as' and the role of the artist as interpreter, designer, commentator and innovator has led to a proliferation of style and movements that provide a dizzying array of possibilities and opportunities, concerned with concepts, processes and communicating journeys of inner/outer discovery.

The perspective of the child has been honoured and respected by internationally respected artists (Klee and Mondrian, among others) for its freshness of vision and simplicity of approach, ironically during the same years as researchers were trying to find out what was 'wrong' with the way in which children drew. There is only something 'wrong' if there is only one 'right' way to represent the world. The multi-purpose images that children first produce are as good a starting point as any for the multiple uses of drawing and the many genres that children will need to learn to read and to produce both throughout their education and in informal contexts. Looking carefully may include analysis of social conventions, learning new cultural norms, developing empathy, responding to the glories of the natural world or examining the preconceptions within their own minds.

In summary of the exploration of what it means to 'draw to see', words from two of the great masters who helped to set the agenda for Modern Art:

Cezanne: *I have not tried to reproduce nature; I have represented it.*
Picasso: *I do not draw what I see but what I think.*

Who could criticize a 5-year-old for doing the same?

Drawing to know

The fifth dimension of drawing to be explored, 'Drawing to know', is the use of drawing as a way of mapping relationships, whether physical or abstract, geographical (cartographic), mathematical (for example, geometrical and topological) or scientific, enabling the sorting and classification of observations, ideas and concepts about the physical world and supporting the development of cognitive schema to construct broader conceptual relationships. This mapping of the perceived world includes the use of drawing to model abstract ideas and relationships as well as using drawing to explore and represent the position of objects in space.

On the surface, this requires a very different sort of understanding of the role of drawing from that explored in the previous dimensions, 'Drawing to see', that is, if 'Drawing to see' is seen as producing camera-shots of the features and objects within the observed world. If, however, the word 'see' is taken at a broader level, to mean to understand, analyse and assimilate, then the kind of 'Drawing to know' that is explored in this chapter can be regarded as a logical extension of that seeing. The diagrams that contain relational and conceptual knowledge, that form the main context for this chapter's discussion, are abstractions and yet even quite young children can access them, both to read and to produce their own. Mapping may support physical, metaphorical or symbolic journeyings. Drawing is a powerful tool for supporting such learning and thinking.

Our discussion begins with one of the oldest forms of visual mathematics, which is as much to do with plotting movement (loci) as it is to do with recognizing properties of shapes:

Geometry

[The universe] is written in the language of mathematics, and its characters are ... geometric figures without which it is humanly impossible to understand a single word of it; without these one is wandering in a dark labyrinth. (Galileo Galilei, quoted in Pappas, 1999, i)

... there is not one geometry but several. (Holt, 1971: 23)

The Association of Teachers of Mathematics (1982) defines geometry as an *awareness of imagery* and algebra as an *awareness of dynamics* acting on that imagery. Both these viewpoints are closer to the real work of many mathematicians (Euler, Gauss, Newton, Mandelbrot) and physicists (Einstein, Bohr) than the reliance on grasping numerical algorithms for calculating arithmetical solutions of traditional and even, unfortunately, much contemporary primary school mathematics. The stunning visual effects created by Mandelbrot's fractals appeal to our senses, yet these are linked to the development of chaos theory which has enabled mathematicians and scientists to begin to understand such diverse phenomena as the movement of clouds, evolution of species and predictions of stock market trends.

Some teachers, however, do not appear to appreciate the important role of drawing in developing children's mathematical thinking:

GH to Year 6 teacher: I'm writing a book about using drawing across the curriculum and I particularly need some maths examples from older children. Do you think I could come to your school and collect some examples or do some activities with the children?

Year 6 teacher: They don't do drawings in maths in Year 6. I suppose in the younger years, in Key Stage 1, they might.

Whatever success the UK National Numeracy Strategy (NNS) may have had in raising standards in basic arithmetic, it has succeeded in blinding some teachers to the fact that mathematics is a great deal more than number bonds and algorithms. Even before the introduction of the NNS the place of measuring weight, capacity, length and area had shrunk into a corner, with the study of space (including symmetry, tessellation and topology) disappearing down a black hole in the skirting board. One problem is that geometry relies on a visual way of seeing the world, and the traditions of Western academic culture have promoted the abstract in preference to the concrete, through seeing mind and body as two different and opposing realms. Lakoff's (1999) *The Embodied Mind* provides a philosophical critique of this position.

Although this duality is based on ancient Greek thought, much of their mathematics was based on geometry. Their numerical system, especially in the handling of fractions, was not sufficiently flexible to support abstract number theory. Greek mathematics is best known to us through Euclid's geometrical treatises, which remained unchallenged for two millennia, before Gauss, Reimann and Euler invented new geometries that led to developing notions of hyperspace and multidimensional multiple universes, which in turn became foundational to contemporary scientific development and exploration. Other ancient

Greeks invented the calculus 2000 years before Newton and Leibzig, whose great leap forward was to transform it into numerical formulae that could be used to describe and calculate the great principles that underlie the workings of the universe. In turn, these numerical techniques enabled the development of computers that could solve ever more complex formulae and display the results on screen so that we can manipulate visual simulations as if they were the real world. Unaware of the formulae behind the display, we use on-screen graphics as tools for design, research and fun.

Even a quick glance at a book such as Pappas's (1999) *Mathematical Footprints* shows just how visual mathematics really is. Every topic is illustrated with pictures and diagrams: wave theory, fuzzy numbers, nanotechnololgy, Cubism, knots, mazes, longitude, chaos theory and Fermat's Last Theorem. The link between mathematics and drawing is ubiquitous. Using drawing as a way of expressing, explaining, developing and generating mathematical thought, therefore, is not just for the very young who cannot yet use standard numbers and symbols, but is an essential part of developing deep understanding, representing and manipulating the physical and abstract relationships of the world around us. The essence of mathematics is to create generalized models of phenomena that have predictive value across a wide range of specific situations, frequently developed visually in the mind of the mathematician, expressed diagrammatically to enable the development of algebraic formulae that will encapsulate the relationships in a way that can be manipulated for a range of variables, both numerical and symbolic.

Understanding geometrical concepts begins with intuitive concepts of size, shape, distance, angle and movement. Developing the basic language of geometry needs to be done with reference to the real world, through first-hand observation and through pictures and photographs. Images that focus on specific parts of flowers and seed heads, on geological strata and geographical features, the patterns made by stars or the trace of light beams from car headlights, all build children's awareness of the geometry of the observed world. Recording observations of geometrical relationships through drawing will begin with the simple:

- Can you draw me a big dog? Bigger than that little one there?
- Can you draw five girls at the bus stop, each one a little taller than the one in front?
- Can you draw a triangle, a square, a rectangle, a shape with six sides?
- Draw a line 10 cm long.

- Look at the picture of Emma watching the television. Draw an arrow to show which way and how far she must turn her head to see her Mum coming through the door.
- Robert is playing on his swing, draw a line to show the path in the air that he moves through as he swings backwards and forwards.

Each of these examples requires a growing sophistication both in the child's understanding of the world and of their ability to transfer that understanding to paper. In the last example, even small children know from experience that they swing up high and down low, but drawing that movement requires the ability to abstract and generalize their personal experience and observation. It enables the child to see the connection between swings in the playground and other objects that move in an arc (conkers on strings, skipping ropes) and to see arcs as parts of circles.

Drawing around objects in order to feel the path or locus of a point moving around the perimeter of two- or three-dimensional shapes is an important prerequisite for more formal geometrical analysis later, since the act of doing is a much stronger stimulus to learning than the merely observing or even handling. The tactile experience of taking a pencil around the shape confirms the straightness or curvature, the length and orientation of each side. Following the locus of points around the outside or inside of a shape requires personal involvement in the path taken. The feel of drawing round the inside of a cut out shape or stencil is different to the feel of drawing round the outside. Children need to do both.

The relationship between the static shape and the tracing of loci is well illustrated by the following case study, an account by an MEd student expecting to observe a mathematics lesson in a secondary school and included in the Association of Teachers of Mathematics' *Geometrical Images* (1982). In this case study (pp. 26–7), it transpired that the class's usual teacher was unexpectedly absent and the college tutor accompanying the MEd students volunteered to take the lesson, only to discover the cupboard was locked, leaving only a piece of chalk and a blackboard for teaching aids as the class of 12–13-year-old boys trooped in. Not a situation that one would imagine to be the source of inspirational mathematics.

The pupils were asked simply to close their eyes and imagine a line, then a circle floating down and resting on it. The circle was to roll along the line and they were to follow a point on its circumference with their mind's eye:

Pupil: I've come to the end of my line.
Tutor: What will your circle do?
Pupil: Go underneath ... sort of roll along the bottom.

The tutor asked him to draw his line and circle on the blackboard.

Tutor: What happens to the point on the circumference now?

Some of the class closed their eyes to look at the picture, others turned to the back of their exercise books and started to draw.

Discussion ensued: 'Most of the class were now drawing, borrowing coins to roll along the line. Arguments arose … pupils began to move around the classroom showing others their results and looking at the contradictions.'

Next, the pupils were asked to imagine their circle rolling around a square, a triangle, inside another circle: 'By now, everyone was engaged in some exploration. I noticed that like me, most of the other students had given up looking at the pupils and were sketching on pieces of paper. Incredibly, I noticed how theorems seemed to be flowing from the study, theorems concerning angle-sums and sums of exterior angles … '

The pupils' engagement, their desire to prove their theories to each other, their intuitive and natural use of drawing to image and develop their own thinking and to support their theories in arguments with their friends, are all noteworthy, including one boy's declaration: 'I'll do it on my spirograph tonight.' This lesson would have stayed in their minds long after the memory of many other lessons had faded. They had been taught to use their imaginations to explore mathematical concepts and had naturally used drawing as an extension of their mind's eye. They had discovered the power of drawing to support and extend their mind's eye and imagination. They used drawing as and when they needed it, to fix the image, to trace a path that they found difficult to envisage, and to test the inner image in the external world.

The fact that this case study is of slightly older pupils than those that we teach in primary schools does not, of course, undermine the principle of the importance of visualization, supported by drawing, for understanding geometrical relationships in the real world. For instance, the following activity to stimulate Year 3 children's thinking about rotational symmetry was linked to looking at the rose window in the church next door to the school. The children folded a circle of paper in eight and attached this to a thick card base. A straight-sided irregular shape was cut from medium-weight card and anchored through one corner to the centre of the circle with a thumb pin so that the card shape rotated freely. The children aligned another corner of the shape to one of the folds, drew around the shape, rotated it to align with the next fold, drew around it again and repeated the process until the shape was back again in its starting position. The card shape was removed and the children identified the repeating symmetrical patterns they had created.

Colouring them in bright colours linked the activity to the rose window they had observed on the local church. A technically more challenging task would be to make a slit in the paper and attach the shape with a split pin so that it could be moved along and drawn around. Marcel Duchamp's (1912) *Nude Descending a Staircase* exploits this positional symmetry for a sophisticated exploration of space, time and higher dimensional mathematics in the pursuit of artistic expression.

Symmetry and asymmetry are two of the most significant definers of our universe. The big bang probably occurred because of a singularity of asymmetry before/within the a priori singularity which existed before/within the big bang. Everything in our universe is almost symmetrical but not quite. Humans have abstracted symmetry from the observations we make of the world around us. We exploit it in patterns to decorate ourselves and other objects, to construct buildings, bridges, tools, furniture, clothes and almost everything else we have created. We seem to have an inner need for symmetry, whether of movement, rotation or the mirror image. Children are highly aware of these symmetries but at an intuitive level. To move children's appreciation of symmetry beyond the human world and into the space/time symmetry of the natural world, opening leaf buds could be traced around on several days in spring. The time symmetry of the seasons, the annual growth, maturation and eventual fall and decay of the leaves as part of the cycle of the year and a sense of continuity through the ages and into the future can be appreciated by children by such hands-on experience. Measurements of such phenomena can be plotted on graphs, which are, of course, just another form of drawing.

Graphs

The visual representation of numerical data through graphs, charts and figures greatly assists understanding and analysis and is of application across all fields of science and mathematics. The ambiguity of the word 'graphic', to describe anything that is drawn, conflicts with the tighter, mathematical textbook use of the word 'graph', to mean a diagram with two perpendicular axes conventionally labelled x (horizontal) and y (vertical) which cross at an origin at 0 on each axis. This is a Cartesian coordinate graph (named after its inventor René Descartes) and can be used to help children sort and classify numerical data from a young age.

Pictograms can be taught to and used by Key Stage 1 children to record basic data such as 'How do we come to school?' or 'Our favourite snacks'. The use of squares of coloured sticky paper instead of drawing the objects or children makes a simple transition to bar charts or histograms. A considerable amount of information can be read from them that may not be obvious from the raw data. Traffic surveys conducted over the course of a week, for instance, reveal trends and anomalies much more readily from the graphical representation than from a list of numbers. Line graphs are more sophisticated and care must be taken to ensure that the children understand that bar charts are for discrete entities (cars, biscuits, and so on) and line charts are for incremental changes (temperature changes during the day, for instance) since the continuous line is enabling modelling of intermediate states between actual measurements. This is quite a sophisticated concept for children to grasp and is best left until the end of Key Stage 2. Pie charts are popular with children. They like the name and can understand readily that each segment represents the proportion of each category. They are too hard for children to produce accurately by hand and should be produced on a computer. Scatter graphs make interesting displays but should be left until Year 6 as they are probably the most difficult for children to interpret. Graphs with multiple axes stemming from a central origin are also useful, especially for demonstrating relationships between several variables.

All these kinds of graphs can be used to enable thinking about mathematical and scientific ideas and information, and have a ready application in geography and science as well as in mathematics. The distribution of resources, rainfall, population and so on often appear in atlases and geography textbooks as graphs. Even if they cannot understand the information, some children are fascinated by these from middle childhood and will spend time poring over the charts as well as the maps. Computer programs that create charts and graphs from arrays of numerical data offer a range of graphical formats and upper Key Stage 2 children (age 10–11 years) can enjoy experimenting with displaying their data in various forms and deciding which is most useful for clearly representing the information. These programs often have 'three-dimensional' graphs, which give a false sense of solidarity to the data. However, familiarity with these various visual forms enables children to understand their use across a wide range of topics, both in the sciences and humanities.

Polar coordinate graphs, on the other hand, are the kinds of diagram that people draw to give directions to others to get from where they are currently standing to somewhere else without recourse to a printed road map (which is plotted onto a Cartesian grid). This intuitive and effective system is used by highly competent non-Western peoples to navigate across deserts and oceans using only the stars and environmental features observed along the way. Polar coordinates have come of age and back into fashion in the computer age with Global Positioning Systems (GPS) using them to display routes on electronic route-finder equipment. Polar coordinates are also used in the same way in computer and video games. The gamer steers right and left through the maze or landscape, using intuitive polar orientations.

LOGO and other similar educational software utilize polar coordinates in a similar way. The procedures that children build are based on movements of the turtle from its current position in order to plot routes that will enclose mathematical shapes or build pictures. The software becomes a powerful thinking tool through naming and storing the procedures, which can then be combined with other procedures. Children can build libraries that can be combined to draw quite sophisticated pictures or mappings. Papert's (1980) book, *Mindstorms*, was more visionary than practical and his insistence that the children could discover mathematical principles by themselves without the teacher, who seemed always to be several steps behind the children in his mastery of the package, did not help to change pedagogy. LOGO is powerful and of real value in the classroom, especially in Years 5 and 6, but teachers often do not have sufficient hands-on knowledge of it or of what it can do.

LOGO can be used to explore the properties of shapes and symmetry, but children need time to build up a shared library of procedures and routines that may not have any relation to mathematical analysis of geometry. The children in Papert's account spent many hours exploring the program; far more than would normally be available within the confines of the overcrowded curriculum. Like all new skills, children need time to play. They also need to be shown the tool's potential, including examples that are not too far beyond their starting point. How to change colour and line styles need to be taught early or the children's interest will quickly wane. It is a program that needs to be added to the children's repertoire after they have experience of working with other graphic packages that produce effects more quickly but give less control to the user.

Concept mapping

The plotting of ideas and relationships that spread out from a single central idea are variously called concept webs, mind maps, spider diagrams and so on. The term 'concept plot' seems to cover all of these diagrams, and be the one that might prove most useful. Books that describe a whole range of diagrams that may be used in different circumstances are sometimes sold under the banner of 'accelerating learning'. What they are doing is teaching children to objectifying their conceptual understanding through creating visualizations and employing graphics to support their thinking about specific topics. Underlying the genre is the general premise that many different kinds of problems have the same relational form. Since the essence of genius is to perceive a common form in two or more apparently incompatible, conflicting or divergent data-sets, ideas, concepts or areas of knowledge, it is argued that if children can be taught the basics of relational mapping, then their thinking will be so much the more powerful.

Many of these devices are genuinely helpful in supporting the categorization of problems and of simplifying them into known forms. Bruner (1979) cites Weldon's assertion that the essence of problem-solving is the ability to convert the problem into a puzzle form that is already familiar and for which a solution or methodology is already known. Using graphics to model these puzzle forms is a powerful strategy. The Venn diagram, the mind map and other graphic forms described above all fall into this category. Children can begin to appreciate the power of these kinds of diagrams as analysis tools through such activities as designing board games and using tree diagrams to represent the rules and choices. Tree diagrams are also commonly used to represent the structure of websites, and Key Stage 2 children may find it helpful to plan out the links between their pages with pencil and paper before creating the hyperlinks on screen. They can then check that the links they make via the keyboard conform to their intentions.

Providing children with a range of graphical techniques for clarifying, analysing and seeking solutions to problem scenarios enables them to see common forms within apparently diverse situations. These graphical devices (which form part of the foundations of systems analysis) can be taught to children, even though their perception of the potentials of this systematic way of thinking will be limited. They will begin to perceive commonalities across puzzle forms and they will acquire a graphical vocabulary and diagrammatic toolkit that they can learn to apply across many different disciplines and areas of knowledge. It may not accelerate learning, but it will enrich children's cognitive capabilities. They will have a greater range of 'containers' in which to store their understanding and ideas.

Topography

Connected graphs are an arrangement of points (*vertices*) connected by lines (*edges*), which are often unfamiliar to teachers and appear less often in mathematical schemes of work, since they do not look like traditional mathematics and so arouse suspicion. However, the graph theory which is based on them is fundamental to solving many day-to-day problems, from organizing traffic flow to designing elec-tronic circuitry. There are two basic forms of the problems that con-nected graphs can solve, each associated with a famous mathematician: Euler and Hamilton.

Euler's seven bridges of Koenigsberg

The city of Koenigsberg is built on both sides of a river, which has two islands. Bridges go from the banks of the river to the islands and another bridge connects the two islands to each other (as shown in Figure 5.1). Is it possible to walk around Koenigsberg and cross each bridge once, but only once? The Hamiltonian path demands the visit-ing of each *vertex* (each part of the town) once rather than each *edge* (the bridges) as in the Eulerian path.

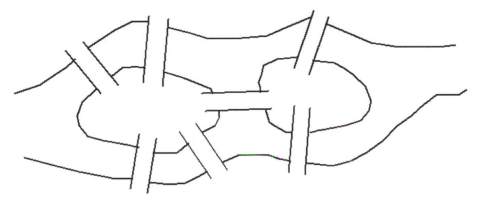

Figure 5.1   Euler's seven bridges of Koenigsberg

Solving puzzles such as this are far easier done with a pencil on mul-tiple copies of the problem, but allowing children to realize this for themselves develops their appreciation of the importance of recording their thinking and strategy development than to simply hand out pho-tocopied sheets with multiple copies of the problem. Figure 5.2 shows Year 4 children using matchsticks, string and short lengths of pipe cleaner in a sand tray to try to solve Euler's bridge problem. They were intensely involved in the group activity for about 30 minutes, by which time individuals were leaving the group and fetching paper and pencil to record their attempts. By 45 minutes they were beginning to put forward theories: if there was an extra bridge here, if you could also go from one side of the river to another, and so on. The children who did not reach for pencil and paper were still randomly trying out new

Figure 5.2 Year 4 children attempting to solve Euler's puzzle

and repeated ideas, convinced they could solve it imminently, if only they could have one more try. The pencil and paper recording of tries enabled those children to quickly see that they had exhausted all variations of possibilities and to look at changing the puzzle: 'What Euler should have said was where they needed to build a new bridge if they wanted to go right round' (Lee-Anne, age 9).

Graphical puzzles of this kind are common around the world and once children's imaginations have been captured by one, they readily embrace other forms (Ascher, 1991). There is an especially strong tradition of graphical puzzles in sub-Saharan Africa, which would begin to provide an alternative view of the region and a greater respect for its peoples than would be portrayed through simply focusing on their current endemic poverty and health problems. The Bushoong of Northern Angola have complex decorative patterns that are associated with status and political power. Each is a continuous planar graph and must be drawn in a particular way. The Tshokwe people come from a similar geographical area, but their graphs (called *sona*) are used to illustrate community stories, especially those connected to the initiation rites of passage from boyhood to manhood. The *sona* shown here (Figure 5.3) demonstrates that the boys are in the camp (central row of dots), with the guardians (upper dots) away from the intrusion of neighbours and other uninvolved people (lower dots).

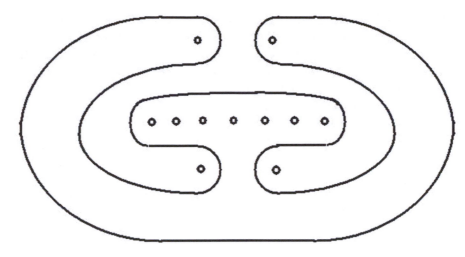

Figure 5.3   Sona design from Northern Angola

Children can be encouraged to devise stories that can be illustrated by *sona* to develop topological awareness, logical thinking and visualization skills. The kind of sophisticated graphic thinking underlies the study of topology, a branch of mathematics that was not much studied in Europe before the late nineteenth century. Playing with abstractions of physical relationships in this way is a complex and powerful means of thinking that is more common among peoples who roam across large open spaces than among those who remain settled in one place.

Complex drawings in the sand, called *nitus*, are used by the people of Vanuatu in the Pacific to denote privilege and position in society and to ensure safe passage to the Land of the Dead. These are passed down from generation to generation within the privileged group. Knowledge of the correct method of drawing them is kept secret from those who have not yet attained any particular level in society. Many of these *nitus* are extremely complex, and all need to be drawn by following an exact procedure and demonstrate a strong sense of symmetry as well as spatial geometry.

These topological puzzles appeal to the human enjoyment of the interplay between complexity and symmetry that we recognize in the natural world. Visual analysis of the trunks of palm trees, seed heads of sunflowers, the complexity of a pebbled beach, the satisfaction of waterfalls and fountains, all seem to appeal to an affective appreciation of symmetrical complexity, in a similar way to our response to complex patterning in music.

The best known topological heritage within European traditions is that of the maze, which is linked to the study of loci, movement and paths of the kind that fascinated Euler and Hamilton. Many stately homes grew mazes (Hampton Court, for instance) but this was based on a much more ancient and complex tradition, of which the story of Theseus and the Minotaur has come down to us. Mazes can be found in unlikely places, including the floors of churches, illuminated manuscripts of the Celtic tradition, as well as being used as defensive devices in castles and forts. Corn mazes have become increasingly popular as this may provide the farmer with as much money as the value of the crop. Some schools have grown their own willow mazes and children enjoy designing and creating their own small grass mazes in school gardens.

Young children may spontaneously use drawing to create, record and communicate movement, routes and paths (for instance, Figure 2.1). This skill can be encouraged in the early years/Key Stage 1 classroom through mapping out routes for toy cars or people in a sand tray. Providing small buildings, trees and other simple props relates the activity to the kind of play in which young children are already experts. Older children will enjoy making town maps, and they too will enjoy the use of props. This can lead to making mazes that conceal and defend, a genre with which children are familiar through computer and video games. Information and communication technology (ICT) tools exist which can be used to create on-screen mazes with virtual props, but children should first have experience of creating mazes with things they can physically handle. Drawing a maze with a short stick in a tray of sand has the advantage of experimentation being invited by the temporary nature of the medium. Although able to understand and solve simple mazes at quite a young age, children below Year 4 find constructing successful mazes quite difficult since they do not appreciate the balance needed between hiding the route from first sight and it being possible to solve. Working in pairs, swapping mazes with a partner and providing peer review and feedback can be helpful.

Cartography

The kind of creative small-scale map-making that underlies the creation of mazes, road layouts for toy cars or even arranging toy furniture in a shoe box are all part and parcel of the playing with space relationships that prepare children to understand the drawing of maps.

Cartographers have to make decisions about:

Scale: how large are the objects that an observer can see in comparison to their distance from the observer?

Position: how far apart are objects that an observer cannot see at the same time from where they are standing? Where are these objects in relation to each other and to other objects, both visible from the observer's current position (A), to one to which the observer can move and maintain a similar viewpoint (B), and one which presents a totally different viewpoint (C) from either A or B and to which the observer cannot travel?

Movement: how can an observer tell if the objects are standing still, moving together, apart, towards or away from the observer?

Representation: how can the observations be represented on paper or computer in a way that will be usefully meaningful to others?

These questions are more pertinent for makers of maps of the universe than for those mapping school yards but they were also important to the early cartographers in sailing ships and a discussion of the map-makers of earlier times can be fitted into studies of the Greeks, Romans, Tudors, Stuarts or Victorians. Mercantor, whose projection of the world map is in use today, had the basic intention of making a shipping chart, enabling sailors to find their way around the globe. His problem was to help sailors on a sailing ship know how they were moving with respect to the coastline they were observing. The whole subject of the historical development of cartography is fascinating and makes it clear that:

- cartography was never, historically, an exact science but always an approximation to reality
- cartography has, from ancient times, been as much a political activity as to do with measurement.

Map-makers make choices, most often based on the function of the map, the scale, the needs of the client and, of course, their own level of knowledge (or ignorance). When studying a particular era of history, children can also study the maps that were made at that time. For instance, when studying the Tudors, they can look at the maps that guided Drake around the world and try to find out answers to questions such as:

Where did he get them from?
Who drew them?
How did they know if they were right?
Was he going to places for which there were no maps?
When were maps drawn of these places?
Why is Australia missing?

Maps are abstractions that ignore the perceptual information given to us by our eyes that enable us to judge distances, as the photograph of a view from Toronto's CN Tower shows (Figure 3.3). Even from the world's highest free-standing building, we see the sides of buildings not just their tops. Maps plot footprints, not real objects with height and depth. Instead of our visual perceptions, maps substitute a Cartesian grid onto which distances and shapes are plotted. Most adults with experience of reading maps could draw a map of the area of downtown Toronto in Figure 3.3 quite easily from the photograph, using their knowledge of the genre of map-making with which they have become familiar through teaching and/or experience.

Matthews (1992: 151ff.) cites evidence of children as young as 3 years old being able to interpret such aerial photographs. In his discussion, he suggests that small toy play, especially involving toy cars and buildings, enables children to take a bird's eye view. This ability is further enhanced through playing with floormats with road layouts, which introduce very young children to the conventions of road maps through playing with older friends or siblings. For instance, children in a British nursery setting, who referred to the railway lines on a map by the name of the make of toy train set owned by the nursery (Matthews, 1992). The tendency of boys, rather than girls, to favour this kind of townscape play may contribute towards the folk psychology hypothesis that men are better than women at map reading and orientation in strange place. They may just have had more practice of practical mapping at a young age.

Matthews (1992) toys with the idea of an inherent mapping acquisition device to parallel Chomsky's language acquisition device, working together with a mapping acquisition support system to parallel Bruner's language acquisition support system (Matthews, 1992: 75). This idea has some currency. Matthews supports his claim with reference to young children's apparent natural skill in depicting the world around them in words, drawing and mapping. He quotes Blaut's suggestion that these are phylogenetic skills, 'inherited by all infants', and Chomsky's comment that infants point before they can speak. In adaptive biological terms, it is more important for a baby to point to danger before needing to name it and it is a frequently observed phenomenon among adult that the pointing instinct will still work when the stress of the moment obliterates the recall of the words to name the horror or danger. That this primeval pointing instinct should transform itself into the ability to produce maps, even without the equivalent development of language, seems not unlikely. This may go part way to account for the exceptional drawing talents of autistic children such as Stephen Wiltshire (1991).

Andy's 'map' (Figure 2.1) might also be cited in support of Matthews's argument. Andy's use of the term 'map' to describe what he had drawn reveals several layers of understanding. First, that a drawing that shows where you go is called a 'map'. Second, that this drawing represents the spatial arrangements of places of importance. Third, that maps have words on them to denote what these places of importance are. Despite Andy's attempts to write words (which may have been assisted by an adult; this is not known) he was still functionally a pre-reader and suffering from delayed language development when he 'read' his map to his teacher some 18 months after drawing it. Given that the context for the drawing was an interview with the special needs coordinator due to his inability to express himself in language, it is unlikely that he would have been able to explain to an unfamiliar adult the content and function of his drawing at that time, aged 4 years. Yet he displayed so much understanding of mapping.

When presented with an aerial photograph and asked to trace the outlines of the buildings, children as young as 4 years were able to discuss the picture in terms of roads and buildings (Matthews, 1992: 157). Thus they were able to make the conceptual leap between the photograph and an abstract representation. Matthews strongly criticizes conventional wisdom, based on Piagetian stage theory, that children below age 7 should not be shown or taught to make maps because they are not able to make sense of them. Piaget believed that children passed through three stages in their developing understanding of space: topological (with self as reference point), projective (with reference to other people or objects) and Euclidean (with reference to external fixed angles, distances, and so on, that form the basic features of conventional Western maps).

These assertions have been the subject of much criticism and reworking by researchers whose gut feelings were that there was something awry here. This 'something awry' was not to do with the procedural reliability of tests as conducted by Piaget. Through setting up the tests differently, using tasks that make 'human sense' to the child (Donaldson, 1979), the validity of Piaget's findings have been questioned. The social constructivists hold the theoretical key to the problem: Piaget's tests reveal the measure of acculturation of the children into Western map-making, as epitomized by Descartes' interpretation of Euclidean geometry, which became the cornerstone of post-Enlightenment education, especially in French-speaking countries. As a man of his age, Piaget's underlying cultural assumptions were that children naturally and biologically progressed towards the ways of seeing and estimating space that was current in his society in his own time. He seems to be either unaware of or to discount other cultural ways of seeing and representing the world, among which we might list topological and projective representations as valid and effective means that adults use to represent the world.

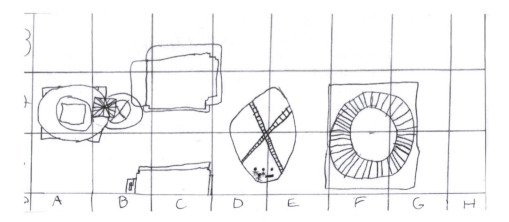

Figure 5.4 A 9-year-old's map of downtown Toronto, based on Figure 3.3

For instance, the Melanesian navigators do not work to Euclidean Cartesian systems any more than do the Inuit or Australian Aborigines, and yet these peoples possess humanity's most advanced capabilities for travel across apparently featureless places unaided by technological support. In Piaget's cultural milieu (and even until recently) these peoples would have been considered by Western societies as 'primitive' and their intellectual achievements denigrated. In each of these three societies, children are treated indulgently and a mixture of informal and formal tuition about navigation takes place, girls equally to boys since lives depend on it. These people would not, however, score well on Piaget's three mountains test. The view of a doll seated on the other side of three toy mountains is irrelevant to a Melanesian navigator. The skill is to know where you are now and where the ocean is taking your boat. For the Inuit, there might be fog or a blizzard on the other side of an Alaskan mountain, so the important skill is to know whether or not to go there at all.

There is nothing biologically determined about the way in which these skills develop. There is, however, a cultural determinism in education and a skill in judging what will be useful to the child at their present stage of knowledge, experience and maturity. When considering developing children's mapping skills, therefore, we must look beyond a quasi-biological determinism towards being able to interpret and draw the kinds of maps that are produced by surveyors (atlases, road maps or town plans). Figure 5.4 shows a 9-year-old's attempt at turning the photograph of Toronto (Figure 3.3) into a gridded map. These are important representations of the world's surface but children younger than age 10 find them difficult to read and draw. Children need to look at different sorts of maps and discuss and understand the

Figure 5.5   Part of 7-year-old's 'Route to School' map

maps' purposes and target audience to enable them to make decisions about the kind of map they will make to convey the information that they want to show.

Picture maps, with houses and trees in side view (for example, Figure 5.5) are not simply an immature stage of map-making that will evolve later into the abstract kind that are published in traditional world atlases. Many cities (including Toronto) publish tourist maps, complete with side-views of important and interesting places to visit, colour-coded (shopping, heritage, sport, and so on) with legends providing details of each. Just yards from Stratford-upon-Avon train station, for instance, is a machine that sells tourist trail maps for £1 that highlight the main Shakespearean and other historical buildings and shopping arcades. There is a tourist map of Canterbury that is 'medieval' style, as befitting its pilgrim heritage. Other towns and family attractions adopt a more disneyesque approach. The London Green trail is adorned with smiling children, cute animals and so on to indicate 'family fun'. Travelling around Paris on foot is most usefully aided by two very different maps. *Paris Monumental* is a large fold-out map with pictures of all the places of major and minor interest for instant reference and planning of the day, with a more detailed and mathematically accurate version on the reverse, which also shows Metro stations. However, *Paris par Arrondissement*, the street-by-street guide in booklet form, is more useful once out and about.

Confusingly contradictory messages about map-making and drawing are given to children. They find themselves being expected to produce more photo-realistic drawings and paintings of their observations of the world for art, to use a different set of conventions of labelled drawings for science and, at the same time, to learn to produce more abstract cartographic schema as 'maps' for geography. Specifically, children are expected to have 'moved on' from the canonical drawings that they produced at age 5–6 (that were not valued because they represented an inner schema rather than the world as seen) and draw the world around them in a more photo-realistic style, yet, by about age 9–10, they are expected to learn and internalize the generalization and abstraction rules for cartographic representation based on the application of a stylized schema rather than the observational moment.

These contradictions are invisible to adults who have come to terms with them. Historically, the roots of the development of both perspective painting and of cartography in Europe in the Renaissance period were in the rise of humanism as a human-centred world view. The art and cartography of the Medieval period in Europe was God-centred. The great cathedrals of the West and the Byzantine gold-leafed frescos of the East both proclaimed the timelessness of eternity. Early cartography was oriented on Jerusalem as the eternal city of God, a concept far eclipsing its association with the historical life of Jesus. Almost as a reaction to the sense of lost-ness among so much eternity, artists began to restate the place of humanity within the world order. The development of perspective landscape painting and navigational chart-making were part of this reorienting of the Western world view (Tuan, 1977). Perspective painting showed a human-eye view of a specific scene. Navigational charts enabled people to travel away from and return safely to Europe to trade with more people and discover new lands on Earth, rather than navigate their way through life to heaven.

Ironically, the more abstract a map becomes, the less relevant is the observer's topological viewpoint and the less human-centric it is. It is not just someone else's projective viewpoint, nor even everyone else's view, but no one else's view. Paradoxically, says Tuan (1977: 17) it is 'God's eye view'. The child, in the Western tradition of cartography, has to accept that they no longer have any input to the view of the world that is shown on the map. Maps show what was important to the map-makers' purpose.

This has obvious implications for a refugee whose homeland has been absorbed by the map-maker into enemy territory, but it also has implications for an islander whose island is too small (Fair Isle, Eigg), or too far away from the mainland (Shetland Islands, Scilly Isles), to be considered worth showing in its correct position, or too close to the mainland to be shown as an island at all (Isle of Sheppey). By being left off or misrepresented on the map, places such as Sheppey and Shetland are denied their important place in the nation's heritage and history, yet both places have been of vital strategic importance in our naval history. Misrepresenting or omitting such sites of heroism from the map devalues the history, heritage and place of a community within the nation.

Children may, understandably, be offended at cartographers' choices and yet their own choices and representation of their choices of what is important is often undervalued in turn. Maps are political, not neutral, documents. Maps accustom and inculturate children into the particular world view of their community, nation and race at a particular time in history. By upper Key Stage 2 (ages 10–11) children can begin to understand this. They can see the straight lines on maps of Africa or the USA and appreciate how land was divided up, not by agreements between local people but by surveyors in offices far away that effectively disenfranchised populations and created human tragedies. Learning about the drawing of maps, therefore, is part of learning about history and politics.

Encouraging children to study and draw maps of their own location can be socially and intellectually empowering. Children's sense of place, of belonging to a locality increases with their knowledge of it as they represent socially shared knowledge. As children pore over local maps and find their street, their school, their park, their shops and the corner where they hang out with friends, they see where they live, and thereby where they themselves, fit into the broader picture of district, town, county and nation: 'I am here. My house is here. I am part of UK; London' (recent immigrant from Sudan, age 10).

This can cascade into practical map-making activities, especially if the school site has a good range of interesting features which cannot all be seen from one viewpoint. Young children's drawings of their route to school are fascinating and revealing of their perceptions of the features in the local environment that they believe to be significant. Buildings that would be expected on an adult map may be missing unless they stand prominently on a corner. The school attended by the Year 2 child who drew Figure 5.4 is next door to a Working Men's Club that allows parents to use its large car park. This car park frequently appears in maps of Key Stage 1 children's route to school, but the club itself does not. There is, unexpectedly perhaps, little difference between the maps of children who walk to school and those who come by car, and one of the most detailed and accurate maps from a Year 1 (age 6) child at this school was produced by a child who travelled a considerable distance by car to school each day. Even the petrol station by the roundabout about 2 miles from the school was included. The least detailed maps were most often produced by children who lived close to the school and walked through one or two roads of houses. Adults looking at the maps displayed on the classroom wall without knowing where the children lived would often pick out 'good ones' on the basis of the numbers of features, and discount the one drawn by the child living opposite the school gate who showed 'my house' and 'the school' linked by a single line.

The immediate environment outside this school's gates is a frequently used resource for geographical study. The main entrance is on a side street close to a crossroads with a cluster of shops. Few children except those who live in the triangle of its immediate streets realize the shape that these roads make, especially those who come by car from the opposite direction, who are barely aware of the connection between the shops at the crossroads and the location of the front gate of the school, since they enter and leave by the side gate. They know about the shops because these are located at the point where their parents turn left to drive to the town to go to the supermarket but have little awareness that they have passed the road that their school entrance is on. Staffroom criticism of the children's lack of knowledge of the configuration of these three streets around their school took a bizarre turn when it transpired that some of the other teachers who came by car from the opposite direction were unaware of it too, yet they drove in through the front gate of the school every day.

This example highlights the difference between maps of personal experience and maps of shared knowledge. There is a tendency to downplay the maps of personal experience in favour of those of shared knowledge and to see the former as less valid, less useful and to be left behind as the child matures. The maps of shared knowledge are those that form the culturally agreed maps, whose form and content are taught in school and accepted by the dominant adult community. These are the maps described by Cartesian coordinates and represent the 'God's eye view'. The maps of personal experience are maps of individual orientation in the landscape, based on polar coordination and are essential prerequisites for the maps of shared knowledge to make sense. There is an interaction, a toing and froing of understanding between the two forms. Looking at a street map of an unfamiliar town is a disembodied experience. The main features of the town are identified and the main roads noted. Looking at a map of a well-known place is a completely different experience, as images of the buildings at familiar junctions or features that cannot appear on the map come to mind.

Even maps drawn by arm-waving may rely on this combination of polar coordination familiarity and reference to Cartesian coordinated route maps. A printed map may simply serve as an aide-memoire: 'Ah, I know where it is', and the map book half closes and is waved about in the air, 'you go back to the lights, turn left … when you come to the pub, you'll see …'. The need to construct and communicate directions forces clarity into the inner hazy recollections of sight, sound and movement, which are often the half-formed inner snapshots of the memory of being there. Drawing maps is, as Matthews (1999) argued, a basic human imperative that seems to be part of the distinction between Homo sapiens and other species. Whether recorded by drawing lines in the sand, knotting stones into webs of string, or printing and selling town plans, the traditions of map-making and map-reading are passed down from one generation to the next. The objectification of our movements through drawing has provided a record of relative positions, angles and distances, enabling travel and imagination of travel across ever-increasing areas and space. Making simple maps enables the understanding and creation of more complex maps in the same way as making any tool enables the creation of better tools that will create even better artefacts, both at community and individual level. For children, the drawing of maps, however crude, begins this process.

The fascination with atlases, the enjoyment of video games based on mazes and the desire to go out and explore the local streets all seem to arrive at about the same time in the child's life. The wider world beyond home and family begins to beckon and the need for a commonly agreed system for making sense of it can be grasped, even if poorly understood. By about age 9–10 children can begin to create and read maps based on mathematical accuracy. However, younger children have a less developed understanding of the importance of standardization and the acceptance of agreed systems of communication, although they will be able to recognize familiar shapes such as the map of the British Isles through watching television weather forecasts and may be able to explain accurately how to get from one location to another along a familiar route. Year 6 children can understand and enjoy practical map-making activities that require accuracy of measurement, both of distances and angles. The activity described below was part of a project in the children's final term in primary school to create a portfolio of memories of the school.

The children went outside in groups to map the site. They decided on observation points from which the measurements would be taken, such that at least one specific feature (preferably containing a right angle, for example, a corner of a building) could be seen from more than one observation point. From each observation point, the children measured the distances to the features they could see, and plotted the directions and measured the lengths of the buildings, using knotted string and very large sheets of paper. Back in the classroom, the teacher talked to them about surveyors' and navigators' traditional use of compasses and dividers, and challenged them to make as accurate a map as possible. Each group transferred their measurements and direction plots to squared paper. The children learnt the importance of accurate measurement and triangulation and related this to their mathematical knowledge about triangles. By drawing as accurate a map as they could of a well-known site, they had begun to appreciate the decisions made by cartographers. There were disputes about directions, what could be seen from each point and how far away it was. They had to go back outside and repeat a measurement in order to settle the dispute and make decisions about how to represent more accurately what they knew to be true on the ground. They found that different groups had taken the edge of the building to be in a slightly different place to each other, which compounded the confusion and disagreements. The finally agreed maps were a compromise of all these factors and changed the way the children saw these surroundings for the last time. Not only did the activity teach them about maps, but it imprinted the features of site itself in their memory and in their consciousness in a completely new and lasting way.

Summary

Throughout the exploration of mathematical and cartographical uses of drawing, the discussion of 'Drawing to know' has outlined ways in which children in primary school can use graphical modelling to plot and describe the world around them in analogical and symbolic ways. This kind of drawing supports the development of more abstract ways of knowing the world around them. Creating visual analogues such as maps and charts provides children with powerful ways of representing the world and communicating their knowledge to others. The analysis of routes and paths, linked to the construction of geometrical shape, provides a means of thinking about two- and three-dimensional enclosed space, and about relationships between position and loci. Linking this to algebraic formulae will come much later in their secondary education, but the grounding in Cartesian and polar graphical representation will provide the foundations for this work, without which the ability to later understand such advanced concepts as algebraic analysis or calculus will be so much the harder. If children have a rich variety of experiences of manipulating ideas and concepts through physically representing them on paper during their primary school years, then this form of visual education will supply the power tools of conceptual imagery and manipulation required for even the highest levels of mathematical understanding and creativity.

Developing the use of drawing to support more abstract ways of thinking that are analogies of conceptual knowledge, as this present chapter has described, encourages children to think of drawing as a way of modelling ideas and their interrelational connections through making abstract concepts and relationships viewable, able to be manipulated and moved around as if they were real objects. Making lines and shapes on a page to be the containers of abstract and conceptual information that can be examined, considered and manipulated enables children to move their conceptual understanding forward, to go on a journey of discovery of the relationships between ideas – or go on a literal, physical journey with a map!

Dimension 6

Drawing to design

Piaget, apparently, said that to understand is to invent. The area of drawing within this dimension ('Drawing to design') is to explain the role of drawing for design, invention and innovation. Although the starting point in this chapter and the examples given within it are mostly from design and technology lessons, the use of drawing for inventive thinking includes areas of science and art, as well as all uses of drawing for planning. Developing pupils' meta-cognition is of importance far beyond the confines of the design and technology curriculum but the subject is ideally placed to develop these skills (Kimbell and Perry, 2001). Straddling the arts and the sciences, using techniques, skills and knowledge from both sides of the traditional divide, design and technology can foster creativity, reflexive thinking and develop 'thinking about thinking'. Drawing enables design ideas to become visible in order to be subject to appraisal by self and others.

The kind of drawing discussed in this context is that used as a planning tool for making or constructing something in other media. The finished product, therefore, is not a drawing, but an object made in, say, wood, card, fabric or mixed media. The planned object is frequently three-dimensional, whereas the drawing, of course, exists in just two dimensions. So the skill the children are being asked to learn and manipulate is quite complex: to transfer ideas about an imagined future three-dimensional form into a representation in two dimensions, which they will then evaluate, make decisions about as if it were the real future object, and then use that two-dimensional image as a basis for making the object (which is frequently judged by their teacher by its faithfulness to the drawn form). It is unsurprising, therefore, that many primary school children do not use drawing effectively to develop their own design ideas.

The problem is not simply 'Can the children do the drawing?' but can they model in one medium (drawing) and then make either another model or a product in a different medium which matches, in some essential characteristic, the model in the first medium (the drawing)?

Gentner (1982) employed the term 'structural mapping' to describe this ability, whereas Veale (1999) called it 'conceptual scaffolding'.

Young children appear to display a natural fluency in symbolic drawing, making lines and shapes stand for ideas about people, events and the observed world, combining linguistic and graphic symbols as their under-standing and capability with handling writing and drawing emerges and develops. Yet this fluid interaction between drawing and thinking, which both the very young and professional adult designers appear to find so easy, seems inexplicably hard-won in the middle years of childhood.

Influence of the National Curriculum for Design and Technology

Prior to the publication of the first *National Curriculum Orders for Design and Technology* (QCA/DfES, 1991), there was no research into young chil-dren's use of drawing for design purposes. In the early 1990s, any litera-ture relating to drawing for design by children younger than age 10 appeared to be an investigation into why the children seemed unable to fulfil the curriculum requirements.

It had been assumed that the practices of design professionals were of educational application, and frequently the age of the children is unspecified, for example:

> Graphic representations, in the forms of drawings, graphs and charts, are used to convey the design technology process and its results. The child grap-ples with the difficulty of transferring an idea to a two-dimensional format. Sketching freezes elusive ideas and provides a format for mental rehearsal as the child mulls over possibilities ... Just as a designer or engineer works with multiple drafts, so the child ... the project will evolve, possibly through sev-eral drafts ... a final two-dimensional rendering will capture the resulting changes in the original design. (Dunn and Larson, 1990: 34)

Even books that gave advice to teachers about how to develop designing skills frequently used the blanket word 'children' with no indication of age. For example, Ritchie (1995: 82), 'The ability of children to develop their ideas through drawing needs to be developed throughout the cur-riculum from an early age – so that "drawing an idea" becomes second nature', with the warning that, 'As children get older ... they and their teachers can put too much emphasis on finished drawing quality' (ibid.), again, unfortunately, without indicating the age range.

The 'design' side of the Design and Technology Orders appeared to be heavily dominated by making explicit things that had previously either been assumed to happen inside children's heads, or had not been consid-ered at all in relation to young children's craftwork (as it was previously known). The newness of the subject in the school curriculum, together with muddled thinking about the role of drawing for design and the capabilities of children at this age produced mixed messages about both.

Teachers, let alone children, did not assume drawing to be a procedural design tool prior to the introduction of the National Curriculum. There could be none of Bruner's 'scaffolding' since teachers had little perception of the intricacies of the structure. Yet this unfortunate document became a yardstick against which children's capability were subsequently to be judged. There appeared to be mismatches among what teachers knew about small children, the demands of the document and what researchers knew about designing.

Educational researchers were quick to document and identify the problems. Not surprisingly, many early papers and articles focused on what young children could not do, and whether or not what they could do was what the National Curriculum writers had in mind all along. The lack of research into young children's design skills prior to the publication of the document made its instructions a cause for anger or despair among teachers, and frustration for the researchers who now entered the field. For example, Constable (1994: 10, 13):

> Th[e] inappropriate use of drawing is partly due to the unfortunate linear approach to D&T which is encouraged by numbering the [old] Attainment Targets 1 to 4, thus suggesting that the complete design needs to be 'generated' before making can take place. … I would like to reassure KS1 teachers that this articulation of ideas need not necessarily be on paper …

Constable also highlighted teachers' hazy perception of the role of evaluation, which, again due to the numbered list of Attainment Targets, was seen as the last lesson in the scheme of work. The iterative nature of designing had not been conveyed to teachers and hence was not being conveyed to children. Stables (1992) observed Year 1 children completely ignoring their drawings of a 'home for a spider' once they began making them. Anning (1993) described two 6-year-olds who thought they were giving their drawing to the hamster as a present; they did not see the drawing as a sketch of something they would make. Even in Key Stage 2, similar observations were made. For instance, Samuel (1991) showed that Year 3 children could use drawing to record design ideas but, as the article makes clear, few teachers felt confident as to how to encourage children to do so. Chalkley and Sheild (1996) reported Year 5 children being unclear about how drawing could support designing.

The design side of design and technology lessons frequently became a variant on 'draw three and make one' which children do not see as 'an essential vehicle for channelling thoughts' (Constable, 1994) but which appears to be more of a hindrance than a help to what they see as the real task of making. In the normal course of their lives, adults do not always draw out what they are going to make. In fact, even adult design professionals do not work like this. Baynes (1998) criticized the effort expended in (and since) the National Curriculum on getting children to produce a design drawing and then carry it out. 'We don't know many real designers who work in such a peculiar way' says Baynes (1998: 26) – and children cannot; they do not work on the material in such abstract terms. He cites a bird house drawn by an 8-year-old. The product is very different to the drawing, because she carried on designing as she made it, 'as adult designers do' Baynes adds. He feels strongly that the role of drawing was being undermined by the National Curriculum, by giving it a role which it could not fulfil.

In similar vein, Hennesey et al. (1993) had already criticized what they called the 'ritual' of drawing and refining drawn ideas before children were allowed to begin work with the materials, saying that this drawing was largely meaningless to the children. This research team considered the linear model of the design process promoted via the National Curriculum not only to be a poor model of how people solve problems, but that its imposition on children lead to lack of ownership of the task and did not allow for the way different types of problems are solved in real tasks, often by informal knowledge rather than formulaic procedures. Thus, they conclude, it is hardly surprising that primary school children were unable to access the methodology of this linear model of designing.

Although drawing is part of the design repertoire, it is not a necessary part of something called 'The design process', which seems to be a basic misunderstanding held by many teachers. Drawing should only be used where appropriate to the task and to the age of the children. A basic design fault of the first National Curriculum for Design and Technology was to list and number aspects of design as individual Attainment Targets, which conveyed to non-specialist primary school teachers that this was a step-by-step linear process, rather than a range of strategies which the children should be encouraged to use.

The revised curriculum of 1993 (QCA/DfES, 1993) removed this implied linear process, but separated designing from making, as if people do not design through making. In any case, 'making' is such a weak word, it sounds less important, intellectual and generally clever than 'designing' that it pushes the non-expert to think that the important work is done in the 'designing' and that the 'making' is just what happens afterwards. That insufficient time is allowed for children to do the 'making', while having spent more than a whole lesson 'designing', is still, unfortunately, a not infrequent occurrence.

The current (QCA/DfES, 1999) National Curriculum makes no such distinction, but it has been so ingrained in teachers' thinking that today's new trainees not only enter teacher education institutions bringing this basic misunderstanding with them from their personal experience as pupils, but continue to have it reinforced by teachers in schools. For design and technology tutors in initial teacher education (ITE) institutions, this is extremely hard to rectify, especially considering the few hours allocated to the subject for those students for whom it is not their specialist subject, but who nevertheless will be required to teach design and technology in school.

Modelling design ideas

In design theory, a 'model' is any representation of an idea that is not actually the final product. Thus drawings, maquettes, mock-ups, first attempts held together with sticky tape and string, are all models. Models hold a special place in design processes, as they inhabit a halfway house between the idea in the designers' heads and the reality of the final product. Drawings form an important part of that modelling repertoire.

There is a distinction to be made between *modelling of* and *modelling for* (Roberts, 1992), that is vital for understanding the role of drawing for inventing. A *model of* something, whether a flow diagram or a medieval castle made of wood, is a *completed product*. It is the end, not just part, of the thinking and designing process. To treat drawing purely as *modelling of*, as a way of creating a 'final design' is to place closure on the designing, as if no further ideas should spring to mind once the pencil is put down. Using drawing to support thinking about something that is going to be made later is orientated towards future thought or future action. Adult designers use drawing as part of a dynamic process, a conversation between paper and brain, if you like, that moves towards a point at which it has fulfilled its purpose. *Modelling for* is a *future orientated process*, ideas are generated, developed and communicated to others. Constructing the reality frequently lies beyond modelling the ideas.

The dimension of drawing under discussion here ('Drawing to design') is more specifically *drawing for* rather than *drawing of* than were the previous dimensions, although obviously there has been an interaction of the two throughout. Drawing for invention, design drawing, in this sense, has a different role, however, than other forms of drawing, since its product is beyond the drawing itself. The relationship of the drawing to this final product is as a staging post, a place-holder and development tool for ideas that will be completed in another medium.

Drawing for designing has two audiences: the self and others. The need for drawing for self depends on the complexity of the task. If the task can be solved mentally, either because it is relatively straightforward or involves known methods with familiar materials, then virtually no drawing needs to be done. For example, an experienced tailor making a simple A-line skirt for herself needs do nothing more than lay a similar sized skirt on the fabric, cut it out and sew it together. Making a more complex garment, a tailored jacket, for instance might demand several drawings to clarify and develop ideas for the styling and detailing before this is developed into a full-size pattern for cutting the fabric. Drawing for others depends on the other person's ability to share meaning with the designer. When making dresses for a small daughter, the tailor might draw ideas for her and ask: 'Do you want puffy sleeves like this? Or straight ones like this? How shall we have the neck, square, like this, or round?' If the tailor were designing a garment for an adult client, then the process would need to include much more sophisticated rendering.

Most writers on designing express a certainty about the role of drawing and sketching as an essential component skill for designers, for example, Welch and Lim (1999: 136) assert, 'Sketching is a form of thinking and the fundamental language of design', quoting Tipping (1983: 45) as saying that sketching ability may be 'the single most important factor in developing any general design ability'.

If these views are correct, then to teach design drawing to children is of vital importance in developing their design capability and inventive powers. Welch and Lim (1999) list the role of sketching as:

- clarifying the task and understanding the design problem
- encouraging the designer to play with ideas without the time-consuming and costly experimenting with real materials
- facilitating evaluation of ideas and identifying and evaluating possible problems
- enabling communication with the self and others 'because sketching is a language'.

However, they discovered that children rarely choose to draw their ideas ahead of engagement with materials. Design drawing in the primary school remains, still, an under-researched area.

In his keynote lecture at the Design and Technology Association's Annual Research Conference in 2001, John Smith raised the following questions:

> If sketching is an important modelling aid for designing then surely more research and curriculum development should be undertaken in how to develop pupils' and students' sketching skills which provide opportunities for ambiguity and hence an opportunity for creating new ideas? What age should learning sketching techniques be started and to what depth? Do pupils understand that one reason for sketching when designing is to assist in the generation of more ideas through the ambiguity of the sketches and the juxtaposition of ideas? (Smith, 2001: 8–9)

Smith provided no answers and quoted no research into this area which might suggest appropriate answers. One assumes that he considered these questions still to be open and unresearched. The remainder of the discussion of 'Drawing to design' attempts to provide some answers.

To deduce from children's enjoyment and facility with other genres of drawing that designing on paper or using drawing to invent something that will actually work is something that they can do without specific teaching makes assumptions about children's understanding of the potential and purpose of drawing for designing. Although ideas are flowing while a child is drawing a picture, in the child's mind the completion of the drawing concludes the event. Understanding that a drawing could be a plan to make something else or that drawing could be used to develop ideas about something that might be made with real materials, is not the same as drawing to portray either real or imaginary events, characters or objects. Many children of primary school age draw amazing machines, buildings and so on, that are highly inventive, but there is no intent to turn these drawings into real machines, buildings or whatever. Thus, although they are producing imaginative drawings, they are not producing *design drawings*.

The research literature on children's design drawings is slim. The overwhelmingly greater part of research into children's drawings is into drawing *as a finished product*, rather than into drawing *for intent to make*. As Outterside (1993) commented, of the three major forms of modelling (iconic, symbolic and analogue) identified by Baynes (1989), only the development of the first has been extensively documented. Bridget Egan's doctoral research had indicated that even Year 6 children did not understand the role that drawing could take in facilitating the flow and development of design ideas (Egan, 2001). My own doctoral research (Hope, 2003) confirmed this, but I found ways to enable children to understand the use of drawing for designing, and this section of the book is drawn heavily from that research.

Without specific teaching at a younger age, children appear to have a mental block on the idea of using a drawing as a blueprint for making a product until around age 8 years. Before this age, most children see a drawing as a picture that has no bearing on the making task for which they have been told it is to be the plan. The potential of the relationship between drawing and construction needs to become conscious in order for a child to see that a particular drawing can equate to a possible answer, and only one among many, to a design problem. This requires a level of meta-cognition and reflexivity in relation to the drawing, which is why the ability to treat drawing as a modelling tool emerges at about the same age at that which children become self-critical about their drawing abilities. Once a child begins to be unhappy with their drawings and says 'I can't draw' this is a marker for the emergence of the meta-cognitive capability essential for using drawing as a design tool. The potential of drawing is no longer seen by the child just as a symbolic representation of their observations and feelings, but as needing to represent locational observations or possible reality. The desire to locate the picture in a setting, leading to the inclusion of weather details (sun, clouds, rainbow, and so on) in children's pictures is often one of the indicators of the emergence of this trend.

Between ages 4 and 7 years, children's ability to imagine a whole scene is developing rapidly and they are learning to use drawing to support their pictorial imagination. This, in their view, is the role of drawing. At the same time, they are honing their skills at putting their inner image onto paper, and mastering techniques and conventions. Their motivation is to produce a complete picture of something. This for a while hampers their ability to use drawing as a drafting tool. They do not want to produce rough unfinished sketches or to have several 'wrong' ones on the same piece of paper, and they are not easily convinced that this is 'showing your thinking'. It is more helpful to provide a pile of small sheets of rough paper that can be stapled together at the end of the lesson than to use a 'design sketch book' for generating initial ideas because children want to put 'best work' in a book. Apart from those who regularly use drawing to develop design ideas, perhaps because they have an art or design background, adults feel the same.

A wise teacher should accept the child's viewpoint about their initial attempts at sketching the ideas they have in their head. A record of 'where I went wrong' is not what a child wants preserved. They will more happily start each idea on a fresh sheet of paper, but may vehemently deny ownership of their first discarded attempts. These are more likely to be screwed up and thrown in the bin and the idea that their teacher wants to keep them may inhibit the child from having multiple attempts in future. The stage of understanding the usefulness of this audit trail of idea development comes with the understanding of the importance of thinking about thinking and making one's own thoughts visible to oneself. This appears to begin between ages 8–10 years. Although younger children can appreciate the usefulness of drawing to develop their ideas, they are less likely to review and combine ideas from several previous drawings without support.

Figure 6.1 shows an example of work by a 7-year-old boy, Craig who was one of the most articulate and design-conscious children in his class. 'That's me drawing,' he said, indicating the pencil. He had previously been observed pointing to part of other children's drawings and making comments such as 'What you could do is …' (Hope, 2003) and making suggestions for the solution to the design problem based on

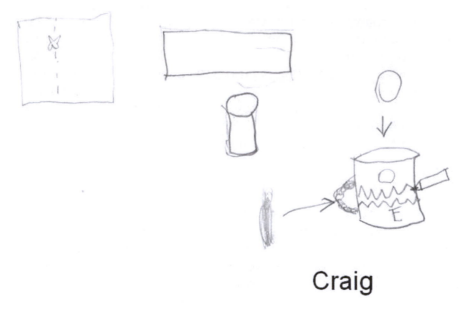

Craig

Figure 6.1   Craig's design for an Easter egg holder

what they had already drawn. Having realized he could read other children's drawings in this way, he was able to apply the same skill to his own output. Figure 6.1 has captured the transitional moment.

The problem at a younger age appears not to be whether children can do the drawing but whether they can model in one medium (drawing) what they would like to make in a different medium (card, fabric, recycled resources) which, in essential but abstract characteristics, matches the symbolic, drawn model. This requires a level of analogical maturity. Even infants will use a person drawn on paper, and cut round, as a character in their play. As children begin to draw they are substituting a two-dimensional symbol for their observed, remembered or imagined three-dimensional image. However, to go that step further and use drawing as a substitute for manipulating real materials and create a two-dimensional image that can then be translated into three-dimensional reality requires a maturation of the child's analogical reasoning that is beyond many children in Key Stage 1.

Younger children (below age 7 years) do not necessarily make a connection between what they can draw and what they can make with other material. They are not seeing the analogical link between the drawing and the future real product. They will follow their teacher's instructions ('make a drawing of what you want to make') but the drawing does not inform their making unless they are supervised and reminded that this is what they should be doing. The children may be well able to draw an idea of what they would like to make and they may be able to see that someone else's drawing is a plan for action, but the joining of the two, the conceptual difficulty, seems to be in seeing that their drawing could become a blueprint for *their own* actions which can be changed and adapted as they think about their future actions *as they draw*.

The conceptual hurdle to be overcome in order to use drawing for designing or inventing something involves understanding the analogical nature of the drawing in the design situation, to see drawing as modelling. To use drawing as a design tool involves imagining that the drawing were the real object and being able to image the product through the drawing, evaluate it, re-image, redraw, re-evaluate and so on, iteratively. It is the messy and interactive nature of design drawing which needs to be conveyed to children.

This is how Lakoff and Johnson's (1980) example metaphors *Container* and *Journey* came to be so useful in explaining to a class of Year 2 (ages 6–7 years) children the role of drawing for designing (see 'Introduction: Drawing to think'). A drawing (as product) is a container, regardless of complexity and stage in the thought process that it supports. Drawing (as process) is a journey, especially in designing, as one's ideas travel across several iterations. To design a complex artefact or invent something new, ideas need to be put into a 'container', a means of objectifying inner thoughts (all those half-baked ideas and fuzzy images) then taken on a mental 'journey'. And just like an infant with a plastic box of bits and pieces to keep them amused on motorways and in aircraft, the contents of the 'container' are to be taken out, played with and added to for the whole duration of the 'journey'.

Key Stage 1 children can see drawing as a one-off recording process, a *container* for their ideas, but not, without help, as a 'modelling for the future' process because they have not grasped the *journey* metaphor in relation to drawing, which involves the sophistication of seeing first attempts as staging posts towards a final solution, rather than as 'wrong' and therefore to be thrown away. To use drawing for inventing, it is the developing ideas not the perfection of the drawing that is paramount. This goes against the desire of young children to be able to produce their 'best' drawing as the final result of the drawing activity.

Frequently, however, it is somehow expected of children to pick up an understanding along the way of the purpose of drawing for designing through being asked to do so, but they are unlikely to extrapolate this abstract process concept and use it efficiently if its purpose is not explained and discussed. Children cannot second-guess the generative and iterative role of using drawing for designing and inventing. However, the 'journey' concept can provide release from the 'I can't draw' problem, because the

drawing in this instance is not required to perform a role beyond supporting the development of their ideas. Children will spontaneously use writing in combination with their design drawings, for instance by labelling
('That's meant to be … but I can't draw it'), listing possibilities instead
of drawing each one, writing the intended colour rather than colouring
the drawing, or writing the intended materials rather than trying to make
the drawing look as if the intended product were made out of them. The
final product, made in another medium, bears the burden of the child's
expectations in regard to realism, but the drawing is relieved of the pressure
and given a clear non-locational role. Design drawing values the recording
of the child's imagination, the externalization of the inner image, in a context replete with realism.

Children can begin to use drawing as a fluid tool for imaging, developing and communicating ideas when their drawings begin take on an
abstract reality of their own, no longer tied to the particular thought
or object that inspired them, but able to be changed, used, tampered
with, crossed out and obliterated because the drawings can be seen just
as waymarkers, not the end of the journey. Using drawing for design
and invention involves a secondary level of symbolic manipulation.
The primary level of symbolic manipulation is to encode and decode
symbols (a word for an object or a drawing for a mental schema). A
deeper level of cognition is required to manipulate these symbols, to
be able to interact with the symbols and enter into dialogue with them
to create, not just new symbols, but a new experience of reality. Until
a child has grasped the idea that drawing is symbolic and can become
context-free, rather than simply iconic, then they are unlikely to be
able to use drawing as a design tool. They may be able to make realistic models and even be 'good at drawing' in the representational sense,
but until they see that ideas about things they will make can be developed by drawing or from the drawing, then this use of drawing is
closed to them.

The purpose of drawing for designing

The missing key to children's inability to use drawing to support their
designing was identified by Egan (1995) as being a lack of understanding of the role or function of drawing within designing. She
found no deeper understanding within a class of Year 6 children than
among a Year 1 class. This might, perhaps, have been due to the small
sample in her research, but is probably symptomatic of the larger picture within many schools. Of the kinds of drawings that might be
related to the use of drawing for designing, Egan observed that:

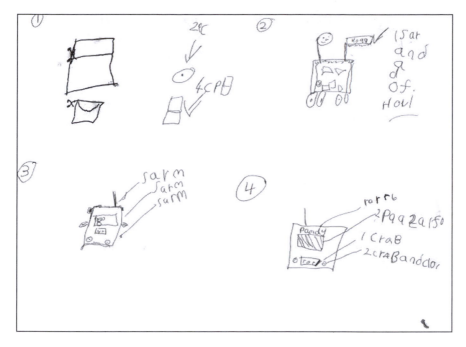

Figure 6.2   Year 2, structured design drawing

certain approaches or intentions while drawing would lead more naturally into design modelling than others. ... Design drawing ... is drawing to explain rather than to depict, and as such has more links with the narrative ... It is possible that concentrating on the pictorial reinforces the concept of the drawing as an end in itself. (Egan, 1995: 9, 14)

Children of primary school age tend to see a drawing as a product rather than a process for generating and developing design ideas. Their agenda for the use of drawing is mastering the genre of conveying three-dimensional objects in a two-dimensional medium while also creating pictorial balance on the paper and aesthetic pleasure in the colours and lines. Constable (1994) described a design drawing as needing to be a simple line drawing, probably annotated, with views from different angles and smaller detailed parts drawn separately, but that few children chose to use the techniques even though they could do them. My own research observations confirmed this and suggested that children as young as 7 years could satisfy Constable's criteria, but only in a very structured task, such as that shown in Figure 6.2, which was in response to a mental manipulation task conducted with two classes from each of Years 1–4 (246 children in total). The children were shown a cardboard box and asked to imagine they were going to make it into a car. They were told to draw side, top, front and back views separately and indicate the extra materials they would need. The children were not asked to make the car and so the detailed plans may not have been perceived as blueprints for making, and they may not have made a car that followed their plans.

From their observations of adults and children (aged 10+), Welch and Lim (1999) concluded that since neither opted to develop their ideas through drawing, that this was not a necessary part of the design process, despite the subjects having been taught isometric drawing techniques. However, they reflected, drawing does improve design efficiency (consideration of options and possibilities prior to engaging with materials of construction) and some of their subjects used drawing to clarify the terms of the task and to establish mutual understandings of a possible solution. From a teacher's perspective, what people do naturally is not necessarily the criteria on which decisions should be made about what children should be taught. On the basis of Egan's research, it could be questioned whether the isometric drawing techniques taught to Welch and Lim's subjects imparted sufficient understanding of the *role* and *purpose* of drawing as a designing tool, or whether this was simply a learnt technique for which the subjects saw no application in the design task.

Teaching children to apply designing techniques familiar in other curriculum areas (mapping, listing and flow charts) is a way forward (Mantell, 1999, referring to the work of Wray and Lewis, 1997), which could enable children to use graphics and text interactively. The Year 2 children on whose work my research focused in 2001–02, showed a much greater level of annotation of drawings than in 1998. The introduction of non-fiction texts and specific teaching of a range of ways in which to record factual information in the National Literacy Strategy for Key Stage 1 seemed to have given children appropriate techniques to use in a Design and Technology situation. The Enriching Literacy through Design and Technology project conducted in the Education Action Zone in Middlesborough demonstrated enhancements in children's ability to record and develop design ideas. Children were encouraged to use drawing and writing to record observations of familiar product and to use drawing and writing to develop their own design ideas. Rogers and Stables (2001) reported that literacy and design and technology had proved to be mutually enhancing.

Egan (2001) worked actively with Year 5 children, encouraging them to record their design ideas through drawing, so that design ideas could be viewed by others, thus enabling communication and clarification through discussion in small groups. After some teacher-led practical tasks to provide knowledge and understanding of materials and processes, the children chose to re-image their ideas and produced more focused drawings of what they intended to make. Again these were older children than those with whom I was working, as were those studied by Ching and Hulsbosch (2001).

Factors affecting children's use of drawing for designing

Figure 6.3 plots the factors that affect children's ability to use drawing for designing. These include external factors, such as the level of support and the nature of the design task, but more important are the practical skills and level of understanding that the children have about drawing to support invention. In this, the children's understanding of the relationship between drawing and making seem to be paramount. Do they understand that they can use drawing to help them *plan* what they are going to make?

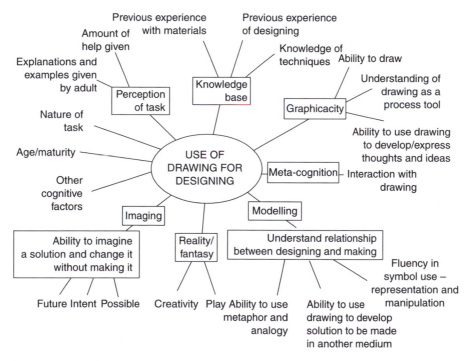

Figure 6.3   Factors affecting children's use of drawing for designing

There is no hierarchy in this diagram, and each or any of the factors may be more or less important at different ages or in relation to different kinds of activities. The discussion begins at the left-hand side, with the age, maturity and cognitive characteristics of the child, and proceeds clockwise to consider the nature of the task in hand, and so on round the diagram.

It is the role and professionalism of the teacher to match the task to the age and maturity of learners, and to take into account the individual's strengths, needs and difficulties. Children cannot realistically be asked to invent a solution to a problem of which they have little experience themselves or which would not be of interest to them. For example, asking primary school children to invent a device to enable an elderly person to live more independently is likely to elicit ideas for labour-saving devices that would leave the elderly person with nothing to do all day except struggle to remember how to work them all. Asking children to devise something for infants or for children younger than themselves is, therefore, more likely to produce realistic ideas. Devising something for their own use or that of a story character with whom they can identify or empathize will get the best response and the most creative ideas.

There is also a difference in the way in which children use drawing to support the generation and development of ideas for a problem-solving activity in comparison to a product design task. If children are asked to use drawing to support the design of a model to demonstrate a solution, they do not use the drawing to record ideas about materials, whereas if they are designing a product, they will think more carefully about the colour and appearance. For instance, Year 3 children (aged 7+) were asked to make models of a maze to help Theseus escape from the Minotaur (Hope, 2004). They were provided with paper to plan the maze and many children used this to clarify the problem to themselves, drawing the kind of maze that they had met in comics, before drawing a plan of something they felt they could make with card. It was clear that the children perceived the card maze to be a *model* of a solution, and that colour, materials and methods of construction were not what they felt they needed to use paper to record. Many of these children had previously produced very detailed drawings for Easter egg holders and greetings cards, as well as travel bags for the class mascot.

There were parallels in their use of drawing in the maze activity with the way these children had used drawing a year previously (aged 6+) to support the development of solutions for making a model from rolled newspaper and recycled resources to show Frosty the Snowman how he could get across a thawing lake to reach Icy's shop on the neighbouring hillside. Thus it would seem that children as young as 6 years old can tailor their use of drawing for invention according to the nature of the task. These findings indicate a high level of sophistication in children's ability to appropriately choose and match their graphic response to the nature of the task than some previous documentation of children's drawings might suggest (for example, Winner, 1982).

Children's perceptions of a task set to them in school by the teacher or other adults is significantly affected by the explanations and examples given by the adult, and the level of help and support subsequently given. Showing children examples of design drawings that show a clear developmental path of idea generation and development provide models of the kind of drawings the teacher is expecting the children to produce. Modelling of design drawing by the teacher or other adult can also be helpful. In both instances, however, the examples shown and demonstrated must not be too far ahead of the capability of the children to whom these are being shown. The aim is to scaffold (to use Bruner's terminology) children within their zone of proximal development (Vygotsky), not to show them something that they cannot understand or attain.

One of the reasons why children's design drawings frequently do not demonstrate the development of design ideas is because teachers do not treat design drawings as developmental documents. Teachers need to become actively involved in developing children's design ideas through questioning and discussing with the child the ideas that are contained within the drawn images, including taking a sheet of paper themselves and starting to draw what the child seems to be indicating they want to make and asking questions about how they want the product to look, how it will fit together, what shape pieces they will need to cut out, and so on. In other words, in order to actively develop the child's graphic awareness and capability, teachers need to model the process in direct dialogue with the child and their innovative ideas. Children appreciate this level of support and discussion. It makes them feel that their ideas are being taken seriously, while externalizing their thoughts and making them more explicit and viewable. The next step may be that the child wants to do more drawing and clarify and develop the idea that has been scaffolded or they may be ready to make the product because the discussion with the teacher has so completely clarified their ideas that they have a complete inner image of what the product will be like. Teachers should not insist on redrawing. The drawing is not the product. It is a drafting medium.

A secure knowledge base of what is possible with the materials of construction is essential for being able to use drawing to model realistic design ideas. When children between ages 6 and 9 years draw their initial ideas of what they will make, they rarely specify the construction technique, and at the younger end of this age band, may not even specify the materials. They are more able to use drawing to generate possibilities than to devise a plan for action. This is largely due to their inexperience with handling the materials. They simply do not know how the final product will turn out. The idea turns into a design in the course of manufacture. It is, therefore, more productive to give children opportunity to experiment with the materials and to learn new techniques before asking them to record design ideas on paper. During the experimentation, the children will produce and discuss possibilities. For instance, a class of 6-year-olds were going to make finger puppets. However, they needed to practise some of the production techniques, notably sewing and fringing, before they started to make the puppets. Design conversations were to be heard around the room, 'Mine's going to have …', 'What I'm doing …', and so on, as they began to realize what they could do and think about how the puppets would look. They needed the direct contact with the materials and techniques in order to be able to make those decisions. When the children have chosen their materials, they are likely to make a detailed drawing of just one single idea. However, if they have not yet chosen their materials, they may produce several ideas or one that is far more flexible in interpretation. Neither approach is better than the other and teachers should provide a range of opportunities for children to develop their imagination and inventive capabilities.

The child's previous experience of designing obviously plays an important role in their use of drawing for this purpose. If they have only experienced the 'ritual' (Hennessey et al., 1993) of 'draw one and make it' or 'draw three and choose the best' they will not be able to use drawing for designing with the capability and fluency of a child who fully understands the role and purpose of drawing as tool for developing design ideas. For my doctoral research, I conducted a longitudinal study, comparing the capability of two parallel classes of children across about 15 months (average age at start 6.2 years, at end 7.5 years), in which the Focus Class received specific teaching on the role and purpose of drawing for designing and the Comparison Class did not. The Assessment Activities (in which both classes took part three-monthly) revealed that the Focus Class children used drawing in a much more powerful way. The Comparison Class children did not catch up with their peers, even a year after the end of the programme, thereby demonstrating that what the children had been taught was not a question of just teaching something that children of this age would soon realize for themselves, but was a direct result of the teaching that the Focus Class had been given (Hope, 2003). Across both classes there was, of course, a range of drawing ability, but what was most significant was the Focus Class children's understanding of drawing as a process tool, which would enable them to generate and develop their design ideas.

How was this difference in capability achieved? It was not by teaching specific drawing techniques but by using the Container/Journey metaphor to explain the purpose of drawing for designing. Three months into the programme, after using drawing to record products at various stages in the making process, the Focus Class were shown two sets of drawings, some of which were design drawings and some not, and asked if they could see a difference between the two sets. After a few moments, one girl asked 'Are those ones planning drawings?' And the others? 'Pictures' said several voices.

The 'planning drawings' were explained as being a bit like going on a picnic.

> You have a bag which contains everything you think you need at the start but then you get along the way and you sit down and get out the things in the bag, eat a sandwich, pick some flowers, repack and carry on your journey. This happens several times along the way. In these planning drawings, you can see how the person drew their first idea, which contained what they thought would work, then their ideas moved on and they did another drawing, and another. This person had lots of ideas so drew them all quickly before they forgot them and then started to think which would be best. This one shows how someone had a good idea but did not like their drawing, so redrew it, but the ideas have not moved on. Two containers with the same idea inside, just one a bit neater than the other. That's fine too, because sometimes you want to tidy up your idea before you can move on. The end of the journey is not on the paper, though. Where is journey's end? Where did the ideas finish up?

'In making something' – Yes!

This was a pivotal moment. The children immediately produced design drawings equal to the best of those produced by Year 3 (age 7+) in a puppet design activity used at the same school with over 300 children aged 5–9 years before the Container/Journey metaphor was developed. Although not all of the Focus Class children were able to maintain the application of this understanding across the wide range of activities throughout the duration of the research project, as a class they demonstrated a far more balanced, secure and growing understanding of the nature of design than the parallel Comparison Class, who did not receive the same teaching input (Hope, 2003).

The vital difference was in understanding drawing as a design process tool, of realizing that the purpose of drawing for designing and inventing is to record, model and develop ideas that will be made in another medium. Through the teaching input they had realized that 'planning drawings' and 'pictures' were two different genres of drawing. Whereas pictures were complete in themselves and expressed everything someone wanted to show about an event, character or object, the role of a 'planning drawing' was not to look attractive in itself, but to support and enable thinking; first drafts of ideas about something to be made in the future with real materials. There was also a sense of liberation about drawing, in that children were able to develop their own ideas and without being judged for their lack of neatness or even the accuracy of

Figure 6.4   Megan's design drawing

their pictorial representation, because these were thinking drawings, waymarkers on a journey to somewhere else.

Showing an active interest in their drawings and discussing their developing ideas with them made the Focus Class children much more aware of their thinking. Figure 5.1 in Dimension 5, showed how one boy consciously recorded his thinking. He has demonstrated how he had thought of two ideas and rejected one in favour of the other. Likewise, Megan's design drawing, Figure 6.4, demonstrates an awareness of the thinking process, including putting measurements on the drawing, linking them with arrows to show the progression of her thinking.

A key result of this understanding of the role of drawing for designing was that the Focus Class discussed their ideas at planning stage, using the drawing as a means of generating ideas and developing possibilities in discussion with each other. The drawings became discussion documents. The children would say to each other 'What I'm going to do is …', indicating their drawn ideas, or 'What you could do is…', pointing at each other's. Using drawing to make design ideas explicit encourages such meta-cognition by making the ideas public and open to view, review and questioning as to whether the ideas can work, crystallizing thought and confirming or disallowing innovative possibilities.

This was in stark contrast to the Comparison Class who frequently drew their ideas in near silence. In the Assessment Activities they tended to simply draw one idea and then ask to make it, as if the drawing were a permission ticket to start the real activity of designing through making. Their finished products were less likely to address the needs of the user or the demands of the task that they had been set. Interestingly, they also showed a less creative range of solutions, despite having demonstrated more inventiveness in activities at the beginning of the programme (Design a Pizza and the Snowman's Shopping Problem) that were used to establish the comparative capabilities of the two classes.

Encouraging discussion over the drawings gave the Focus Class children instant access to other children's good ideas as well as keeping each other on task. This sharing of good ideas at the planning stage did not occur in the Comparison Class and so they each had a more limited set of ideas on which to draw and they were far more likely to veer off-task once making. On one occasion, one girl in the Focus Class (Nikki) had the idea of making pop-up rabbit's ears in the lid of her Easter egg holder. This idea subsequently appeared, not only in the work of other girls seated nearby, but in that of one of the boys who happened to be walking by on his way back to his seat on the other side of the room. Central to this Easter egg holder activity was the use of a wide card tube in which a small egg had to be secured, as well as making the holder attractive for the recipient. Unlike the Focus Class children, several of the Comparison Class children discarded the tube and found other recycled materials that would fit the egg, thereby substituting the real design problem with one they could solve more easily.

In the final activity of the research, Theseus' Maze, most of the Comparison Class used drawing simply to draw the kind of maze that would be found in a puzzle book, far too complex to make in the card provided. The real designing began once they were working with the card and then the flights of fancy took over, making staircases and snake pits to trap the unwary Theseus. Their conversations indicated that these constructions were indeed to trap him and not to help him escape. In contrast, the Focus Class had quashed each other's 'off task' ideas at planning stage: 'Will he go up there and round there …?' The request 'Miss, where's the string?' was the clearest indication that the Focus Class children were on task when making their model of the maze. Few children in the Comparison Class asked for the essential piece of string to show the route Theseus should take out of the Labyrinth and some did not incorporate it at all even though directly given it. They were playing a different game to do with creating a maze, not answering the design problem they were given to solve. The Focus Class had learnt to evaluate their ideas against the design criteria at the planning stage by making their ideas explicit through drawing. The Comparison Class had not.

The Focus Class were not taught any specific drawing techniques throughout the programme. It was the concept of using drawing as a tool for thought that was conveyed to the children through using the Container/Journey metaphor. They confidently used the term 'design journey' to describe their thinking process. The choice of the kinds of drawings and the way in which they used them was left for them to decide. Most of the children annotated their drawings and many did use labelled diagrams, either transferring knowledge from science or literacy lessons, without any direct teaching in the design and technology lessons. In the Theseus' Maze activity (at average age 7.5 years) some of the children used legends and keys, which they had been taught in geography.

Through direct interaction with the children, in discussion and in modelling the use of drawing for design and invention, a teacher can enable the children to see the potential of drawing to support the generation and development of innovative ideas. This appears to be something that children at age 7 years will not realize for themselves, although they are capable of understanding and using drawing in this way. It is important that the teacher does not insist that drawing be used to record a completed design with no room for manoeuvre or compare the final product with the last drawing. This is not just unrealistic and stifling of children's creativity, but also fails to acknowledge the way in which ideas continue to develop once they are tried in the real materials. All adults, including professional designers, continue to design and reinvent as they work with the materials and components of the product. A different way of working should not be imposed on primary school children as it will only prove counterproductive.

This is equally true of teaching children specific drawing techniques at too young an age. The Comparison Class, in the study reported above, were taught to make clear labelled diagrams of their design ideas, yet it did not contribute to their ability to use drawing to develop ideas about a product that they would subsequently make. With older children (ages 10–11 years) who have a secure grasp of the fluid use of drawing for designing, the teaching of conventions in order to enable clear communication of their ideas to others may be needed. 'Technical drawing' is an abstract conventional system that takes time and practice to master. Some children will adopt a stylized version of it, gleaned from science or craft books, and this should be encouraged and developed since it aids communication. If children are able to use a wide range of drawing genres, then they will be able to choose a technique that is appropriate to the situation. Using drawing to invent something new, to generate and convey creative ideas, is not possible at the same time as learning a new drawing technique. Graphical ideation fluency, the ability to produce a flow of ideas onto paper, is only possible in a style and genre which has been internalized. Suggesting the use of legends taught in geography, of labelling or cut-away diagrams taught in science, and so on, is more likely to lead to creative inventiveness in the course of drawing than teaching specific drawing techniques (for example, isometric projection). If drawing is to assist the flow of ideas, it cannot be inhibited by struggling with the drawing process itself.

Any sort of drawing can be an analogy for the real object being invented. Drawing exists as a waymarker along the journey between inner hazy image and clear resolution. It can be discussed as if it were the real object that has been invented, so stands as a metonym for the product to be made, both in the mind of the inventor as well as their audience. Both the user and viewer of inventive, designerly drawings engage in a particular and quite specific game of interaction between fantasy and reality. The object being invented is discussed as if it were real, yet the possibilities are still live and dynamic. Design drawing has that 'as if' quality of all drawings, yet it is intentional, future oriented, a lead-in to a work of development and further creativity that has the potential to move on to a form which the drawing has indicated but not fully defined.

Sketchbooks and process diaries

Robinson's (1995) title, *Sketch-books: Explore and Store*, powerfully suggests a dual function for notebooks that are small enough to be taken backwards and forwards between school and home. The essential thing is to ensure that they do! Just giving out sketchbooks at the beginning of the year and hoping that children will enthusiastically fill them is a waste of time and books. Children need to be taught how to use a sketchbook and using it must start in the classroom. They are unlikely to use a book given out at school for their home drawings. These are private affairs and they will not want to fill a school book with them and bring them into school. What they can be taught and encouraged to do is to use the sketchbook in a range of contexts in school and then this may spill over into their use of a private sketchbook at home.

Children are frequently unaware that adults do not produce works of art at first attempt, whether written, visual or musical. Hammond (1997) stresses the importance of young children knowing that redrafting their writing is not just acceptable but vital. The same is true of art and design work. Showing children collections of artists' drawings (for example, Turner's sketches) can enable them to understand the way that great artists went around collecting ideas and making notes. Turner's notebooks are especially insightful. He frequently wrote comments on the sketches about colour (or put a quick dab of colour to remind himself of the tone or hue of the clouds, fields and so on) either right across the drawing or as labels connected with arrows. Turner was cavalier about rearranging scenes to make them more poetic and apparently upset the inhabitants of several towns by omitting parts of the view or adding features from other places to make the final work look better. This kind of information about artists' working practices enables children to better understand the *composed* nature of works of art as well as understanding how the artist collected and collated observations and ideas. This process often took far longer than assembling the final product. Practising artists also spend a lot of time perfecting technique, mixing colours, experimenting with new processes and viewing each other's work. Children need to know that teachers are asking them to do these kinds of things because it is what adult artists do.

Young children often quite naturally repeat and rework images and themes over a period of days or weeks, which constitutes an editing and redrafting of ideas (Matthews, 2002). This might be harnessed to encourage children to maintain a sketchbook. However, teachers' desire to see and assess everything might militate against the genuine use of the book. A book also limits the children's choice of paper and its very format might suggest to children that it needs to be neat and tidy, whereas adults' sketchbooks can be scruffy affairs, likely to contain the shopping list on the same page as a detailed drawing of the corner of a building. Leonardo da Vinci's drawings not only reveal the workings of a brilliant eclectic mind but are a record of the uninhibited way in which visual journals are used by those who think graphically.

A way of tracking the development of Design and Technology projects, Rogers and Clare (1994) recommended the use of a process diary to record design development in a variety of media: words and photographs as well as drawings, to enable children to record and think about the process of design through recording significant moments in the development of their project. Rogers and Clare identified reflectiveness as the most important aspect of this work The children were able to look back over their design process and reflect on the decisions made at various stages. This made children meta-cognitively aware of their own thought processes, which, in turn, informed their future thinking.

Robinson (1995) suggests that children should make their own sketchbooks, and combining this with Rogers and Clare's process diary may be the best way forward, especially in upper Key Stage 2. All sketches, notes and photographs for a specific project (regardless of curriculum area) could be stored (dated) in a document wallet. Children would then easily be able to lay out their different ideas side by side on the table at different stages of the project and use them as a resource as well as a reminder of where their ideas might be going. At the end of the project, the children could review and assemble these sketches, notes, downloads, photographs and so on into a project journal. A frontsheet that stated the aims of the project and a backsheet that contained the child's reflective evaluation of their progress through the process as well as examples or photographs of the final product would complete the journal. Children could also be encouraged to add reflective comments on the various stages of the work represented by each page. These could be written on sticky notes. The aim is not to make the journal into a work of art but into a genuine tool for real reflection on a lived process.

For younger children, practice pieces (or photographs of three-dimensional work), drawings and writing could be stored in a loose-leaf folder. Valuing this record of the process enables children to understand the importance of these activities within the overall project. Time should be given at the end of a project for children to look back over this record and to talk about the process. This does not need to be a whole-class discussion. In fact, more fruitful discussions may be had in small groups, as children share their reflections on the project with friends with whom they feel comfortable sharing their ideas, including those early ones that got scrapped in favour of something that worked better.

Summary

The first dimension 'Drawing to play' began with a story and 'Drawing to design' has ended with one. As stated in the introductory paragraphs to this dimension, the examples are taken from design and technology lessons. This, as has become apparent as the discussion has progressed, is largely due to this being my area of doctoral research. This has also meant that the examples come from the children whose learning was the subject of that research, who attended a first school (ages 5–9 years) in South East England. The implications of the research are that older children would understand the Container/Journey metaphor even more readily than the Year 2 Focus Class (average age 7.0 years at the date of its initial presentation to them). It is also likely that the metaphor transports across subject areas. Design, whether for technology, art or science is the same basic cognitive skill. That the context of this study was design and technology provided its specific focus but its application is much wider. Any area of the curriculum in which children are asked to invent a solution to a problem or design a product requires a facility with using drawing for designing. This is not contained in knowledge of specific techniques but in the facility to take ideas on a journey called designing, using whatever comes to hand in support of the design process.

Children should be given opportunities in all subjects to make the knowledge and understanding their own through being asked to design or invent. This might be ways of attacking or defending a castle, developing their own designs for batik based on studies of Asian textiles, inventing space probes to discover new planets, and so on. It can be a means of combining different subject areas (designing a batik kite) or pushing out the bounds of their understanding. The essential is the personal creation of new knowledge, of new ways of seeing a problem or an opportunity. Each of the dimensions of drawing discussed in this book has this potential; 'Drawing to design' makes this function of drawing explicit. Designerly drawing should become part of the children's drawing repertoire across all curriculum areas.

Finale

Drawing to conclusions

The aim of this book has been to act as a stimulus to further thought, not to be an encyclopedia of drawing practice and possibilities. The intent has been to outline, discuss, suggest and argue for the use of drawing by children as a medium for exploration, generation, development, expression and communication across wide areas of representational and symbolic activity. These have not fitted tidily into curriculum subject areas and even some with well-known identities such as mathematics have had their boundaries stretched to meet with art, cartography and pattern-making. If readers think, 'What about …?' then so much the better.

The subject of drawing has been examined and explored through viewing its different 'dimensions' and how as a 'container' for ideas that are taken on a 'journey' children can record and develop their ideas. These metaphors, used as organization devices, have been employed, not just to bring some semblance of order to a complex subject, but also to express an understanding of the way in which drawing is used. However, this has not always been neat and tidy. Like the wayward thoughts that drawing tries to tie down onto the page, the ideas about drawing in all its forms have sprung out across the dimensions like errant jack-in-the-boxes.

The act of drawing, for whatever purpose is teleological. The impetus is to clarify a nascent thought, to capture a perception, to model an idea. Once these begin to form on the page, the drawing begins to converse with the eye and the mind. Where and how will the next line be drawn? What about the other ideas that are now racing to the front of the mind, which need capturing before they disappear? The drawing appears to be taking form, but how will it be made to look more realistic, express the ideas more clearly, show what has been imagined or remembered?

The questions that teachers must, inevitably, ask are 'How can I help my class do it better? What tips can I pass on to the children? What techniques can I teach them? What can I put in my lesson plans that will enable the children in my class this year to use drawing as a medium for developing thinking and expressing feelings in the ways that have been described in this book?'

The first thing teachers should do is to model the use of drawing themselves. More than 10 years ago, Anning observed that; 'Drawing is not habitually demonstrated [in the classroom] as a useful tool for organizing and representing ideas ... our education system rarely offers examples of adults modelling drawing as a tool for thinking' (Anning, 1993: 38). This situation has not changed in UK schools across the intervening period, especially with the introduction of National Literacy and Numeracy strategies, which have increased emphasis on linguistic and abstract symbolic means of representation.

Many teachers do not use drawing themselves in the course of their own thinking, or if they do, they do not realize its value. Teachers have had to use writing as the medium of expression in order to become teachers, even those whose main subject is art or design and who might naturally think more visually. Many teachers opted not to continue their own artistic education beyond the age of 14, already at that age feeling a sense of inadequacy about their drawing skills. This sense of graphical inadequacy, coupled with a high level of success in language-based media, militates against their use of drawing to organize information or to communicate ideas in classrooms.

Matthews (2002) asserts that child art does not develop very far without interpersonal adult support, and this is equally true of all forms of drawing. It is the interactive process that is important. Teachers without a background in art are often concerned about teaching drawing because, they say, they themselves cannot draw. However, as has been explained throughout this book, using drawing for learning and thinking is not about being 'good at art' but about using graphics to support the generation, clarification, development and evaluation of ideas across all curriculum subjects.

Teachers should not decry their own output in front of children. This conveys to the children the message that a drawing that they perceive as so much better than their own is not good enough by some unstated, arbitrary and external criteria, rendered in the vernacular as 'not looking like the real thing'. Teachers do not do this with other subjects. They conceal their own confusions with mathematics and they read books to learn facts about history and geography, grasp basic and specific scientific concepts, and take home paper and card to practise what they want the children to make in design and technology. They are multi-talented, highly motivated lifelong learners.

Such anxieties are misplaced since teachers are not required to demonstrate drawing, and to do so would limit children's own creative responses. As Cox et al. (2007: 35) point out: 'It is more important that teachers recognise the difficulties that children might encounter than that they themselves demonstrate the solutions to the problems'. If a teacher wants to show children something specific, they need to practise it beforehand. Everything improves by practice, including drawing.

However, the preceding comments relate to drawing as *product*, a final product that adults always feel is not good enough because they still hark back to the feelings of inadequacy that they felt themselves as children and adolescents. This book is about using drawing as a *process*, to support thinking across the curriculum.

A résumé: drawing as a tool for thought

'Drawing to play' discussed the way in which the youngest children use drawing to objectify and explore the characteristics of the world around them. They make marks simply for the enjoyment of making the marks, but increasingly to play with ideas, patterns and relationships. In order to encourage children to experiment, a wide range of tools need to be available throughout the primary school years. Opportunities to master techniques and the handling of specific tools and media need to be part of children's education. Creativity depends on having the *know-how* (as well as the knowledge of facts) to develop thinking. Drawing in a range of genres, styles and media provides the technical capability for playing with ideas. One of the main outcomes of rich play opportunities is the knowledge of how to play. Without this playfulness it is difficult to learn new things regardless of subject matter. To fully master new information, to understand the potential and application of new knowledge, requires the internalization of that information and to connect it to knowledge that is already held. Using drawing for playing with ideas is a powerful means of manipulating complex concepts, expressing feelings, observations and perceptions.

From infancy, humans imbue their graphic output with meaning. 'Drawing to mean' explored the role of drawing in supporting the expression and communication of meaning. This meaning may, like drawing itself, be multifaceted and multilayered, involving emotional, mathematical, artistic and symbolic meaning. The metaphorical, analogical nature of drawing, as an intermediary, a gateway and a door-keeper between the inner world of thought and imagination and the outer reality of the observed world and other people, makes it a rich and powerful medium for generating, developing and communicating thoughts and ideas. The product is the meaning, expressed through form and content.

The act of drawing is often imbued with emotional content. We view a drawing as 'pleasing' if it conforms to our inner view of balance and pattern, or we are disturbed by its jarring elements. 'Drawing to feel' examined the way in which patterning is felt to be satisfying and how the act of drawing can contribute to a sense of personal well-being. Emotions such as empathy, humour and even spirituality can be explored and enhanced through the act of drawing, through the total involvement of a non-linguistic system of thinking, feeling and communication.

'Drawing to see' explored the use of drawing to record observations, yet these are more than the dispassionate recording of observations. All perceptions are filtered through the human mind and via the preoccupations of the moment. Hence, children at different ages express these perceptions differently, and frequently their interpretations of adult requests are not as the adult intended. As in all intellectual and communicative pursuits, the child is using drawing to make sense of the world around them. They are actively re-creating their inner thoughts and ideas, struggling to master unwieldy drawing instruments, refine their technique and in constant pursuit of better means to do so.

The focus of the book then shifted to a different way of seeing: the inner 'seeing as understanding' and using drawing to explore and express relationships both spatial and conceptual. 'Drawing to know' included map-making, geometry, graphs and diagrams. This is the area in which teachers themselves are most comfortable with their output. As an analogue system, the products do not need to look like real objects: symbols, lines and shapes stand for shared understandings of ideas, places and relationships. Children learn to use these at a surprisingly young age, bearing testimony to the inherent human capacity for metaphor and analogy.

Finally, 'Drawing to design' discussed the way in which children can use drawing for invention and innovation. This final dimension turned the book back around on itself to recount how the Container/Journey metaphor came to underpin its thinking and how this was, in practice, a powerful means of explaining to children the role of drawing for thinking, planning and designing.

The six dimensions of drawing are not, strictly speaking, sequential, since each overlaps and contributes to the other. Indeed, it is hard to distinguish one from the other, and several of the examples of children's work have been referred to in more than one dimension. However, there is a suggestion of progression, in that no progress can be made towards effective communication of meaning without previous experimentation, play, with materials and techniques. The playing can be satisfying, leading to exploration of pattern and form, and the process of drawing as well as its product may be expressive of deep feeling. This may be purposeful, part of the intended meaning, or it may be a contiguous result of the process.

Meaning, feeling and seeing (and knowing) are inextricably linked, woven together and often unable to be separated or teased out. The kind of seeing on which the dimension 'Drawing to see' focused certainly entailed all of these. Feelings affect perceptions, which then limit or enhance observation and determine the kind of seeing that takes place. The assumption that seeing precedes knowing is a common-sense viewpoint that is not always accurate but seemed a conventional way of organizing the material, especially since the kind of knowledge being discussed was the more abstract and symbolic kind. Threads that were begun in 'Drawing to mean' and were developed as semiotic and symbolic uses of drawing in mathematics, science and cartography were discussed.

'Drawing to design' drew these threads together. It is not the learning of specific techniques or styles that enable children to use drawing to generate, explore, develop and communicate exciting and innovative ideas; it is simply the knowledge that drawing can be used in this way. It is gaining the understanding that one of the purposes of drawing is not to produce a pleasing picture but to create ideas that will exist in the future or in the imagination or in other materials such as fabric or card or paint. This is one of the most powerful uses of drawing: combining playfulness, meaning, feeling (whether of empathy with a future product user or of aesthetic balance and form), perception and imagination, knowledge of manipulation of the drawing system and of the symbolic nature of drawing, plus the wonderful ideas that can be modelled, developed, evaluated and communicated through lines enclosing spaces on a surface.

Drawing the final product

Despite the focus of this book being to encourage the use of drawing as a process tool, it would be inappropriate to ignore the role of drawing as a final product in itself, especially in the final chapter. Indeed, there have been examples of drawings as final products throughout the book, to illustrate the way that children have used drawing to develop their thinking and to record their learning.

One of Matthews examples (2002: 181, Fig. 116) is a masterly single point perspective rendering of a toy by his son Ben. It is obvious that the boy knows this object well. He has handled it, embraced it, played with and through it, and studied it from every angle. The drawing comes from his emotional as well as his intellectual response to the object. It also conveys a deep familiarity with the object's three-dimensional form and its proportions to such an extent that the object can be readily visualized from the drawing. A rare talent in a 9-year-old, but an important lesson is embedded here. Ben is able to produce such a drawing, not just because he clearly has talent, but because he is drawing an object that he knows intimately. He has handled and studied this object repeatedly from every angle. While playing, he has placed it on the carpet along with the rest of his Star Wars toys and sat, knelt and lain down alongside them and among them. He has viewed this toy repeatedly from every possible angle. He has studied it with the intensity that only a young enthusiast can do. In contrast, children in school are frequently asked to draw things with which they have only passing familiarity or can barely imagine. It is unsurprising, therefore, that children from homes where drawing is not so richly encouraged do not produce such precocious masterpieces as does Ben.

My interest in children's drawings has spanned the past 12 years. My favourite drawing is probably Glen's Klee (Figure 4.1). I asked if I could photocopy it and he gave it to me, freely, generously, to keep. To him it was just one of so many drawings; no more precious than the last or the next. I also like Randall's Theseus on the front cover, which has a vigour and sense of excited potential. I regret not having had a tape-recorder to hand to capture Jason's cat story (Figure 2.2). I like the relishing of exploration of colour, pattern and form in Hayley's butterfly (Figure 3.1). I am impressed by the virtuosity in Andy's chair (Figure 4.3) but sad that this little boy was viewed by others (and increasingly by himself) as not able to access the curriculum in the same way as his peers. Each drawing, in its own way, has a spark of originality. However, there is one child who over several years caused me to question repeatedly what creativity really means. This book cannot end without her.

Zara was, depending how her output was interpreted, either constantly off-task, divergent or really creative. At home, she and her older brother were constantly inventive. For instance, aged 6, she made a hot air balloon which she placed over the hallway radiator in the hope that it would take off. When it did not, her brother fetched their Dad's cigarette lighter, with almost disastrous results. Figure 1.1 showed two large figures that she and her friend Hayley made at her house one evening at about the same time. In school, Zara found learning to read a challenge and her grasp of mathematical techniques was shaky. In Year 1, when her class went for a walk around the school field and brought back blossom and daffodils to draw as 'signs of spring', Zara drew a cross-sectional drawing of how potatoes grow underground. In Year 3, when her class were asked to devise a model of a maze to help Theseus escape from the Minotaur, she devised Episode 2: a model of a river outside the Labyrinth with a crocodile lying in wait and a boat to take Theseus safely across.

Many anecdotes like these could be told about her. Zara's design ideas were always different to those of the other children but she frequently ignored the constraints of the activity as set to the class. The question that always remains regarding Zara and those like her is: how many conformist hoops will she have to jump through before (if ever) her creativity will shine through? Will she fulfil her creative potential and invent something new, exciting and innovative, or will she, unfortunately, slog along in the below-average stream, always below par, never fully engaging in the education process, never quite sure why her thoughts and ideas are not what teacher wants. Could using drawing have helped to channel this extraordinarily fertile imagination into productive creativity? I believe it could. If Zara's ideas could have been shared with others through drawing, perhaps they could have seeded other children's imaginations. Reciprocally, sharing her ideas with those whose ideas flew less far could have brought her back on track and channelled her ideas into the problem in hand.

Ultimately, the products of any educational endeavour are not facts, figures or even techniques, but *people*. Underlying any educational policy, initiative or recommendation lie beliefs about the kind of people and society that their writers believe to be the ideal goal of the process: to be better readers, better writers, better mathematicians, better citizens with more respect, and, occasionally, to be more creative. Yet, never, to be better at drawing.

Undervalued and sidelined as an attractive accomplishment for those who want to do that sort of thing, rather than as a ubiquitous powerful modelling tool for the future, drawing is repeatedly overlooked. However, people who can analyse and communicate complex relationships in a few strokes of a pen are powerful thinkers and communicators. People who can evoke feelings of empathy, understanding and beauty through their portrayal of observations and perceptions contribute to the well-being of the nation. People who can play with ideas and communicate those ideas to others, for evaluation, appreciation, comment and dissemination have, down through the ages, been those who made some of the most significant and innovative changes to the human world. In a global economy and a shrinking world, where shared language cannot be assumed, the ability to manipulate graphics may become one of the most important human skills. It is increasingly the medium of the computerized world, whether as a means of entertainment or in the worlds of work and home-making.

As this book has explained, drawing is a powerful means of learning and thinking, not just as a product of thought, but as a process of thought. It is so powerful that educators may be severely limiting children's ability to think and model complex relationships by not teaching them to draw. The increased pressure on children to be proficient users of written language rather than any other form of communication may be hampering children's ability to think, imagine and reason for themselves. Drawing can provide the tools for thinking, modelling and communicating ideas, concepts, understanding and emotion. It can do so swiftly and efficiently. It can be assigned meaning yet remain open and ready for change. It can make comment through humour, irony and satire. It can move, inspire, speak to the innermost thoughts and feelings. It can model abstract mathematical relationships and communicate complex scientific ideas. To deny children access to this power, simply through neglect, is to deny them a means to contribute to the ongoing creation of human innovation.

In 'Drawing to play' it was observed that a neglected aim of allowing children opportunities to play is to develop their playfulness. Play is not just a means of teaching children other things in a format that they find appealing, but the ability to play is an essential human characteristic, throughout life, not just in childhood. Playing with ideas is one of the foundation stones of creativity. Externalizing thinking, whether through drawing, writing, music or model-making, makes creative thought visible, able to be shared, reviewed, evaluated and appreciated. Drawings contain creative ideas in a way that is clear yet ambiguous, stable yet dynamic. Drawings represent creative journeys, leaving the trace of ideas that have travelled but providing the starting place for the next move forward. In 'Drawing to design', the observation was made that the end-product is frequently not the drawing itself, but a product to be made in another medium: card, wood, plastic or fabric, perhaps. Journey's end, in this case, is off the end of the map.

This said, therefore, rather than the book coming to a ringing conclusion that might bring closure to its readers' own thoughts on the subject, it exits with two related couplets, purposely ambiguous, purposely multi-meaningful, replete with divergent interpretations, applications and implications; tools for thought, containers for further journeys in many dimensions. Two couplets whose interrelated, reflexive questions underpin drawing for learning and thinking in all its dimensions:

Drawing to learn/learning to draw?
Drawing to think/thinking to draw?

Bibliography

Anning, A. (1993) 'Learning design and technology in primary schools', in R. McCormick, P. Murphy and M. Harrison (eds), *Teaching and Learning Technology*. Wokingham: Addison-Wesley.

Archer, B. (1992) 'A definition of cognitive modelling in relation to design activity', in P. Roberts, B. Archer and K. Baynes (eds), *Modelling: The Language of Design*. Design Occasional Papers No.1. Loughborough University of Technology, Department of Design and Technology.

Aritzpe, E. and Styles, M. (2003) *Children Reading Pictures*. London: RoutledgeFalmer.

Arnheim, R. (1969) *Visual Thinking*. Berkeley, CA: University of California Press.

Ascher, M. (1991) *Ethnomathematics: A Mulitcultural View of Mathematical Ideas*. Boca Raton, FL: Chapman and Hall/CRC.

Association of Teachers of Mathematics (1982) *Geometrical Images*. Derby: A.T.M.

Athey, C. (1990) *Extending Thought in Young Children*. London: Paul Chapman Publishing.

Bailey, E.P.M. (1971) 'The springs of creativity in the young child', in F. Slater, (ed.), *Education and Creative Work*. Hull: University of Hull Press.

Barrett, M.D. (1983) 'The study of children's drawings: Piagetian and experimental approaches', *Early Child Development and Care*. 12, 19–28.

Baynes, K. (1989) 'The basis of designerly thinking in young children', in A. Dyson (ed.), *Looking, Making and Learning*. London: Kogan Page.

Baynes, K. (1998) 'Draw-um paper', in Loughborough College of Art and Design, *Drawing Papers*. Loughborough University of Technology, Department of Design and Technology.

Blanshard, B. (1964) *The Nature of Thought, Vol. 2*. Atlantic Highlands, NJ: Humanities Press.

Bruner, J. (1979) *On Knowing: Essays for the Left Hand*. Cambridge, MA: Harvard University Press.

Campaign for Drawing (2002) *Start Drawing*. Lutterworth: Featherstone Education.

Chalkley, C. and Sheild, G. (1996) 'Supermodelling! Developing designing skills at key stage 2', *Journal of Design and Technology Education*, 1(1): pp. 32–41.

Ching, J. and Hulsbosch, M. (2001) 'Developing design', in *Conference Proceeding, Third International Primary Design and Technology Conference (CRIPT)*, Birmingham.

Coghill, V. (1989) 'Making and playing, the other basic skills', in A. Dyson (ed.), *Looking, Making and Learning*. London: Kogan Page.

Constable, H. (1994) 'A Study of aspects of design and technology capability at key stages 1 and 2', Conference Proceedings IDATER 94: pp. 9–14. University of Loughborough.

Craft, A. (1997) 'Possibility Thinking and What if?' in A. Craft et al., *Can You Teach Creativity?* Nottingham: Education Now.

Cox, M. (1992) *Children's Drawings*. London: Penguin.

Cox, S., Grahame, J., Hearne, S., McAuliffe, D. and Watts, R. (2007) 'Art and design process', in S. Cox and R. Watts (eds), *Teaching Art and Design 3–11*. London: Continuum.

Csikszentmihalyi, M. (2002) *Flow*. London: Rider.

Damasio, A. (2003) *Looking for Spinoza: Joy, Sorrow and the Feeling Brain*. London: Harcourt.

Dewey, J. (1978) *Art as Experience*. New York: Doubleday.

Donaldson, M. (1979) *Children's Minds*. Harmondsworth: Penguin.

Donaldson, M. (1992) *Human Minds*. Harmondsworth: Penguin Books.

Dunn, S. and Larson, R. (1990) *Design Technology: Children's Engineering*. London: Falmer Press.

Edwards, D. (1993) *Drawing on the Right Side of the Brain*. London: HarperCollins.

Egan, B.A. (1995) 'How do children perceive the activity of drawing? Some initial observations of children in an infant school', *Conference Proceedings IDATER 95*. Loughborough: Loughborough University, Department of Design and Technology.

Egan, B.A. (2001) 'Drawing for designing: the development of purposive drawing in children during the primary school years', unpublished PhD thesis, University of Southampton.

Eisner, E.W. (1972) *Educating Artistic Vision*. London: MacMillan.

Emig, J. (1983) The *Web of Meaning. Essays on Writing, Teaching, Learning and Thinking*. Upper Montclair, NJ: Boynton/Cook.

Eng, H. (1931) *The Psychology of Children's Drawings*. London: RKP.

Fèvre, L. (2004) *Contes et metaphors*. 2nd edn. Lyon: Chronique Sociale.

Freeman, N. (1980) *Strategies of Representation in Young Children*. London: Academic Press.

Fournoy, V. (1985) *The Patchwork Quilt*. London: Bodley Head.

Gardner, H. (1984) *Frames of Mind*. London: Heinemann Educational Press.

Gardner, H. (2007) *Five Minds for the Future*. Cambridge, MA: Harvard Business School Press.

Gentner, D. (1982) *'Are scientific analogies metaphors?'*, in D. Miall (ed.), *Metaphor: Problems and Perspectives*. Hassocks: Harvester.

Gick, M.L. and Holyoak, K. (1985) *'Analogical problem solving'*, in A.M. Aikenhead and J.M. Slack (eds), *Issues in Cognitive Modelling*. Milton Keynes: Open University Press.

Goldschmidt, G. (1994) *'On visual design thinking: the Vis kids of architecture'*, *Design Studies*, 15(2): 158–173.

Goodenough, F.L. (1926) *Measurement of Intelligence by Drawings*. New York: World Books.

Hammond, S. (1997) 'Acknowledging the signposts in young children's writing development' unpublished Postgraduate Diploma paper, Canterbury Christ Church University College.

Harste, J.C., Woodward, V.A. and Burke, C.L. (1984) *Language Stories and Literacy Lessons*. London: Heinemann Educational Press.

Hennessy, S., McCormick, R. and Murphy, P. (1993) 'The myth of the general problem-solving capability; Design and Technology as an example', *The Curriculum Journal*, 4(1): pp. 73–87.

Holt. M. (1971) Mathematics in Art. London: Studio Vista.

Hope, G. (2001) *'Taking ideas on a journey called designing'*, *Journal of Design and Technology Education*, 6(3): 53–61.

Hope, G. (2003) *'Drawing as a tool for thought'*, unpublished PhD thesis, London University.

Hope, G. (2004) *'"Little c" creativity and "Big I" innovation within the context of design and technology education'*, Conference Proceedings, Design and Technology Association International Conference (DATA), Sheffield.

Hope, G. (2007) *Taxonomy of a research task: Unpacking the panda's suitcase*. Conference Proceedings. D and T Association (IDATA) University of Wolverhampton: Telford.

Howe, A., Davies, D. and Ritchie, R. (2001) *Primary Design and Technology for the Future*. London: David Fulton.

Jones, E. (1962) '*Psycho-analysis and the history of art*', in E.H. Gombrich, (ed.), *Meditations on a Hobby-Horse*. London: Phaidon Press.

Kellogg, R. (1959) *What Children Scribble and Why*. San Francisco, CA: NP Publications.

Kimbell, R. and Perry, D. (2001) *Design and Technology in a Knowledge Economy*. London: Engineering Council.

Koestler, A. (1974) *The Act of Creation*. London: Huchinson.

Kress, G. (1994) *Learning to Write*. London: Routledge.

Lakoff, G. (1999) *The Embodied Mind*. New York: Basic Books.

Lakoff, G. and Johnson, M. (1980) *Metaphors We Live By*. Chicago, IL: University of Chicago Press.

Lieberman, (1977) *Playfulness*. New York: Academic Press.

Lowenfeld, V. (1947) *Creative and Mental Growth*. New York: Macmillan.

Luquet G.H. (1927) *Le Dessin Enfantine*. Paris: Alcan.

Mantell, J. (1999) 'Teaching designing skills at key stage 2: is there a role for techniques?', in *Conference Proceeding, Second International Primary Design and Technology Conference*. Birmingham: Centre for Research into Primary Technology.

Matthews, J. (1999) *The Art of Childhood and Adolescence: The Construction of Meaning*. London: Falmer Press.

Matthews, M.H. (1992) *Making Sense of Place*. Brighton: Harvester Wheatsheaf.

Milton, S. (1989) *The Art of Jewish Children*. New York: Allied Books.

Outterside, Y.R. (1993) 'The emergence of design ability: the early years', in *Conference Proceedings IDATER 93*. Loughborough: Loughborough University, Department of Design and Technology.

Pappas, T. (1999) *Mathematical Footprints*. San Carlos, CA: Wide World Publishing/Tetra.

Papert, S. (1980) *Mindstorms*. Brighton: Harvester.

Pink, D. (2005) *A Whole New Mind*. New York: Riverhead.

Pye, D. (1964) *Nature and Aesthetics of Design*. London: Barrie and Jenkins.

Qualifications and Curriculum Authority/Department for Education and Skills (QCA/DfES) (1991) *National Curriculum Orders for Design and Technology in Key Stages 1 and 2*. London: Qualifications and Curriculum Authority/Department for Education and Skills.

Qualifications and Curriculum Authority/Department for Education and Skills (QCA/DfES) (1993) *National Curriculum for Design and Technology in Key Stages 1 and 2*. London: Qualifications and Curriculum Authority/Department for Education and Skills.

Qualifications and Curriculum Authority/Department for Education and Skills (QCA/DfES) (1999) *National Curriculum for Key Stages 1 and 2 in England and Wales*. London: Qualifications and Curriculum Authority/Department for Education and Skills.

Raney, K. (1998) Untitled, in *Drawing Papers*. Loughborough: Loughborough College of Art and Design; Loughborough University of Technology, Department of Design and Technology.

Ritchie, R. (1995) *Primary Design and Technology*. London: David Fulton.

Roberts, P. (1992) 'Of models, modelling and design: an applied philoshical enquiry', in P. Roberts, B. Archer and K. Baynes (eds), *Modelling: The Language of Design*. Design Occasional Papers No.1. Loughborough University of Technology, Department of Design and Technology.

Robinson, G. (1995) *Sketch-books: Explore and Store*. London: Hodder and Stoughton.

Rogers, M. and Clare, D. (1994) 'The process diary: developing capability within National Curriculum Design and Technology – some initial findings', in *Conference Proceedings IDATER94*. Loughborough: Loughborough University of Technology, Department of Design and Technology.

Rogers, M. and Stables, K. (2001) 'Providing evidence of capability in literacy and design and technology in both year 2 and year 6 children', in *Conference Proceedings CRIPT 2001*. Birmingham.

Rogoff, B. (1996) 'Developing Transitions in Socio-Cultural Activities', in A. Samaroff and M. Haith *'The 5 to 7 Shift'*. Berkley: University of California.

Rosen, M. (1996) 'Reading "The Beano": a young boy's experience', in V. Watson and M. Styles (eds), *Talking Pictures*. London: Hodder and Stoughton.

Rubens, M. and Newland, M. (1983) *Some Functions of Art in the Primary School*. London: ILEA Inspectorate.

Safe, L. (1985) 'Anomalous Drawing Development' in N.H. Freeman and M.V. Cox *Visual Order*. Cambridge: Cambridge University Press.

Samuel, G.E. (1991) 'They can never make what they draw' in J. Smith (ed.) *Conference Proceedings IDATER91*. Loughborough: Loughborough University.

Schomburg, R. (2000) *Using Symbolic Play Abilities to Assess Academic Readiness*. www.earlychildhood.com/articles

Shiff, R. (1998) 'From primitivist phylogeny to formalist ontogeny: Roger Fry and children's drawings', in J. Fineberg (ed.), *Discovering Child Art*. Princetown, NJ: Princetown University Press.

Silver, R.A. (1978) *Developing Cognitive and Creative Skills through Art*. London: Routledge.

Smith, F. (1992) *To Think*. London: Routledge.

Smith, J.S. (2001) 'The DATA lecture: the current and future role of modelling in design and technology', *Journal of Design and Technology Education*, 6(1): pp 5–15.

Stables, K. (1992) 'The role of fantasy in contextualising and resourcing design and technology activity', in *Conference Proceedings IDATER92*. Loughborough: Loughborough University, Department of Design and Technology.

Stern, W. (1924) *Psychology of Early Childhood up to the Sixth Year of Age*. New York: Holt, Reinhart and Winston.

Tipping, C. (1983) 'Acquiring design skills for teaching – a self-help suggestion. Studies in design education', *Craft and Technology*, 16(1): 12–14.

Toffler, A. (1970) *Future Shock*. London: Pan Books.

Tourengeau, R. (1982) 'Metaphor and cognitive structure', in D. Miall, (ed.), *Metaphor: Problems and Perspectives*. Brighton: Harvester

Tuan, Y.-F. (1977) *Space and Place: The Perspective of Experience*. London: Edward Arnold.

Van Sommers, P. (1984) *Drawing and Cognition*. Cambridge, MA: Harvard University Press.

Veale, T. (1999) 'Conceptual blending', www.compappdcu.ie/~tonyv/papers/CogSci.ps,gz (accessed January 2002).

Voake, C. (1997) *Ginger*. London: Walker Books.

Vygotsky, L.S. (1986) *Thought and Language*. Cambridge, MA: MIT Press.

Welch, M. and Lim, H.S. (1999) *'From stick figure to design proposal: teaching novice designers to "think on paper"'*, *Conference Proceedings, Second International Primary Design and Technology Conference (CRIPT)*, Birmingham.

Wells, G. (1986) *The Meaning Makers: Children Learning Language and Using Language to Learn*. London: Hodder and Stoughton.

Wiltshire, S. (1991) *Floating Cities*. Harmondsworth: Penguin.

Wilson, B. (1993) 'Primitivism, the Avant-garde and the Art of Little Children', in D. Thistlewood, *Drawing, Research and Development*. Harlow: Longmans.

Winner, E. (1982) *Invented Worlds*. Cambridge, MA: Harvard University Press.

Winnicott, D.W. (1971) *Playing and Reality*. London: Tavistock Press.

Wittgenstein, L. (1969) *Philosphical Investigations; The Blue Book; The Brown Book*. Oxford: Basil Blackwell.

Wray, D. and Lewis, M. (1997) *Extending Literacy: Children Reading and Writing Non-fiction*. London: Routledge.

Index

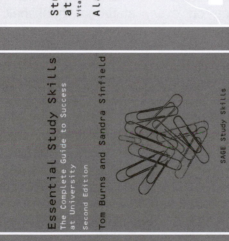

Promoting Reading for Pleasure in the Primary School

Michael Lockwood, University of Reading

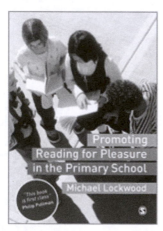

'This book is first class. It puts the matter very clearly and succinctly, and presents a great deal of evidence to support the argument that pleasure is not a frivolous extra, but the very heart and essence of what reading is about. It also gives readers plenty of ideas for carrying the principle into the classroom, and for justifying it...This is an excellent piece of work, which I hope will find a place on every staffroom bookshelf' – *Philip Pullman*

Promoting Reading for Pleasure in the Primary School is written for all those involved in education who would like to see as many children as possible develop a love of reading. It will be particularly relevant for primary teachers, teaching assistants, trainee teachers, advisers and consultants, as well as teacher educators and researchers.

Contents

Introduction / Becoming a 'Reading for Pleasure School' / Promoting Reading for Pleasure in the Early Years / Promoting Reading for Pleasure in the Later Primary Years / Getting Boys Reading for Pleasure / Conclusions / Resources for Promoting Reading for Pleasure

June 2008 • 168 pages
Paperback (978-1-4129-2967-7) £19.99
Hardcover: (978-1-4129-2966-0) £60.00

Find out more and order online at
www.sagepub.co.uk